20/20 VISION

FOR

AMERICA

20/20 VISION FOR AMERICA

CHRIS LASCELLES

SEMAGRAPHE PUBLISHING
GARDEN VALLEY, TEXAS

Semagraphe Publishing
P.O. Box 846
Lindale, TX 75771
www.semagraphe.com

Ordering Information:
Discounts are available on quantity purchases. For details, contact the publisher through the web or mail address above.

ISBN 978-1-7347315-0-7

First Printing 2020

Printed in the United States of America

To those who will lead America
toward her true source of greatness,
with kindness and patience,
yet strength, courage, and truth.

CONTENTS

Acknowledgments

I would like to thank those whose life and teaching have inspired the writing of this book, including Loren and Darlene Cunningham, Leland and Fran Paris, Winkie Pratney, Peter Warren, Bill Burtness, Jim and Barbara Kilkenny, Larry Allen, and Anna Bastounes.

Special thanks to my mother, Sally, for praying for me and encouraging me toward the path of life when I was young. I am very thankful to my wife, Debbie, for freeing up so much time during this writing project, and for giving honest feedback. I greatly appreciate the input of Scott Tompkins, Katherine Ewing, and Annette O'Brien in early stages, and Chris McKinney at Called Writers for excellent assistance in editing and finishing this project.

Above all, I am thankful for Jesus, who opened my eyes to see God, myself, and others more clearly, and who has given a basis for hope and vision for the future.

Preface

A dust cloud formed on the horizon.

"Just a distant storm in the desert," they assured themselves, until the sight of the growing tempest was accompanied by rumbling, like the thunder of a thousand hooves.

Flutters of apprehension rapidly gave way to panic—the unthinkable was emerging before the Israelites as they fled from Egyptian slavery. Pharaoh's horses and chariots appeared like the ghosts of bondage past, pinning the Israelites against the coastline with nowhere to run.

Seeing only two alternatives, death in the sea or a return to Egypt, a chorus of defeat rose up in the camp. "Give us tyranny rather than death!" the people cried, until a voice of hope and confidence broke through the despair.

"Move forward!" Moses commanded the people, as heaven responded with the only thing that would now save them—deliverance by the hand of God. The Red Sea parted. Israel escaped on dry land as Pharaoh's pursuing army vanished beneath the returning waters.

Facing this crisis, Moses knew something Pharaoh and

Israel did not. To Pharaoh, the Israelites had no purpose to fulfill in the world—they were just his property to take back. Moses, on the other hand, knew more was at stake. Was it just that his people might die, or return to slavery? No, it was more than that. Israel had been raised up by God, and called to fulfill purposes that would affect every other nation on earth—a truth they needed to rediscover.

The great escape from tyranny that day has forever changed the world. Among other things, Jesus, the Bible, and the shaping of Western civilization have come as a result of Israel's preservation.

The lesson is this: Our response to the challenges of today affect many generations to come. Abraham Lincoln echoed this idea in reference to the American Civil War and its surrounding issues, saying, "The struggle of today, is not altogether for today—it is for a vast future also."[1] We are also reminded that God brings about history-changing interventions to secure his purposes. Our main job is to cooperate with him, and when the Red Sea parts, to move forward!

America, a nation with its own rich history of divine intervention, is once again being pushed toward a Red Sea crisis. Cultural hostility is raging towards America's Judeo-Christian foundations.

Yet this nation's roots run deep. When revisited and tended to, they spring to life, restoring the understanding that America has been blessed by God to be a blessing to all nations. We have every reason to appeal to heaven for our *Red Sea to part.*

Judges 2:10 says, "and there arose another generation after them, which knew not the LORD, nor yet the works which he had done for Israel."

May that not be said of our generation.

NOTES:

1. Abraham Lincoln, *Message to Congress,* December 3, 1861.

SECTION ONE

America's Foundations

1

Introduction: Missionary to America

Behold, you will call a nation you do not know. (Isaiah 55:5)

"You have got to be kidding!" That's what I thought after the missionary training school students prayed about their field trip options in the late 1990s. I had been working with the organization Youth With A Mission (YWAM) at the Tyler, Texas campus—staffing a transformational program called the Discipleship Training School. YWAM is built on the idea that young people are a vital part of changing the world by taking the message of Jesus to every nation. These students wanted to spend six weeks touring the United States, performing a 13-song musical calling America to prayer, repentance, and spiritual awakening. It was a fantastic idea, but there was a big problem: Only one girl in the school really knew how to sing!

America's Got Talent

However, what happened over the next ten weeks as we prepared to hit the road was amazing. All of us in the school, both staff and students, got intensive voice training. We learned to care for our vocal cords and stay hydrated. Our musical potential was called out and brought to life. People who did not think they could sing grew in confidence and ability. No one was more surprised than me when we finally started to get a handle on the powerful and beautiful musical *Heal our Land,* composed by Jimmy and Carol Owens.

In the weeks that followed, I saw our crew of seemingly "ordinary" young people transformed, as they led thousands of people in worship and interactive prayer—all for the revival of America's spiritual health. Were we perfect? Far from it! But I saw how powerfully America responds when called to revive the deep roots of faith and purpose which have blessed and prospered this nation—making it a beacon of freedom and light to the whole world. Everywhere our team went, we felt like we were pouring water on a wilted plant as we reminded people of the hope we have for reconciliation, healing, and the fulfillment of America's calling to bless the world. I had no idea that was just the beginning of my calling to be a missionary to America.

I've Got Questions

In the early 1990s—while far across the Pacific Ocean—I remember developing a strong yet elusive sense of purpose. "There is something in this world I am supposed to be doing, but I don't know what it is," I would say to myself. That statement describes the preoccupation of my heart and mind as I reflect back upon that time period.

Born in 1970, I had grown up in a remote farming community in New Zealand's North Island. As a kid, life in the country was good. There were rivers to swim in, trees to climb, and in the evening my favorite American TV shows to watch!

Back then, America was as far from my mind as it was from my home. However, I remember a subconscious curiosity about this distant land that seemed to lead the world in so many ways. From Disney Studios to Apple Computers, an endless stream of influence and invention seemed to flow from this country—a place where a garage was not just for parking cars but for changing the world.

Purpose seemed like a pretty straightforward concept during my childhood, except when it came to the subject of God. I felt drawn to something that seemed as real as it did mysterious—like the curious attraction Lucy had for the wardrobe in C.S. Lewis's *The Lion, the Witch and the Wardrobe.* While my parents were not especially religious, from time to time my mother would attend a small church in a neighboring village. I remember always sensing I should go with her, so I most often did go. I could not explain why at the time, but it seemed like the right thing to do.

By the time of my teenage years, things were tough for our family. My father had developed Alzheimer's disease in his 40s, and faded out of our lives. Some good did come out of this time in that my mother's faith strengthened, and my father became a strong believer before his mind slipped too far. He was truly a changed man. For example, once his drivers' license was taken away, he would ride a bicycle to town and visit sick people. Throughout this time I continued to attend church whenever my mother did.

New Zealand's Got Sheep

Upon leaving school, my chosen career was—of all things—sheep shearing. In those days, New Zealand had about 3 million people, and 70 million sheep! Being a seasonal job, it required traveling around the country, and later, around the world. The sheep shearing industry could be a rough environment. Over time, my nominal commitment to God came to hang by a thread.

While paying a visit to my mother, she invited me to hear an evangelist speak at a high school gymnasium. On this occasion, I was not so keen to go, but went to try to please her. That night produced a radical transformation. I remember very little of the message, but will never forget the dealing of God

Figure 1: *Sheep grazing in New Zealand's South Island.*

in my life. As the evangelist spoke, all I could hear was God calling me back to the relationship I had faintly perceived as a child. The choice was clear: I could have my sin and its consequences—or I could have him. I went forward at the altar call and was the last person to leave the counseling room.

During the four years that followed, I continued to shear sheep in New Zealand, Australia, and England. Eventually, I bought a house and the exact car I wanted. I also realized one of my more modest personal dreams—a small workshop with every tool I needed. Besides finding a wife, I had everything I wanted and thought I should be happy. But that's when it began. A sense of calling started to gnaw at me; there was something in this world I was supposed to be doing, but I didn't know what it was.

God's Got a Plan

Once again, I visited my mother. This time, she handed me a cassette tape, saying, "You have got to listen to this guy Keith Green, a Christian musician from the 70s!"

I was not excited.

When I heard "Green," and "70s," in the same sentence, all I could think of was some pot-head hippie strumming a guitar! Still, I put the cassette in my car stereo and hit play.

From the first note of the first song, I knew I had found something related to my quest for purpose. Keith's songs were full of conviction and clarity of calling. He had one song about Jesus commanding us to go into the world as missionaries. When I heard his music, I said to myself, "Whatever he is doing—that's what I want to do!"

I devoured Keith's music and read a book about his life called *No Compromise*. Keith had become well-known across the United States in the late 70s and early 80s, challenging people through his music to love God with their whole lives. But in 1982, at the age of 28, Keith died in a plane crash in East Texas.

The book deeply impacted me. I was left with a radical challenge by a simple paragraph on the last page. It described an "Intensive Christian Training School (ICTS)," in Lindale, Texas, at the ministry Keith and his wife, Melody, had started years before. My heart beat faster as I realized I was experiencing what others have referred to as "The call of God." This opportunity had been placed before me, and a step of obedience was required. I applied to the school and was accepted.

Called to America

As it turned out, the ICTS school I attended in Texas was now being run as a Discipleship Training School (DTS) in conjunction with YWAM. This would prove to be a providential introduction to the organization I would spend many years with. Right from the time I arrived, I sensed a long term calling to America—for a purpose that would unfold in due time.

The training school was a big step toward becoming more mature as a young man and a follower of Jesus. I grew in my identity and character through the dynamic teachings about

God's nature and character, relationships, prayer, and much more.

Like so many foreigners who come to America, I was intrigued by many things. The currency did in fact have "In God We Trust" printed on it. There was a Bible in the nightstand of almost every hotel. So much seemed to point to a past that was rooted in Christian faith. Even the President would conclude a major address with, "May God bless the United States of America."

Delivering the Message

One training school with YWAM led to another. Before long I was a full-time missionary, helping train and take teams to various parts of the world. Although I had come from New Zealand in response to the call of God, I came to realize something over time: I was not viewing myself as a missionary to America quite the way I needed to. It was easy to train people then send them out with a message for another country. But God had sent me to America. What was my message for *this* nation?

It was intimidating to think of having a message for a nation with so many great Christian leaders, such vast Christian resources, and such an amazing missionary history. In spite of this, I began to seek God, to study the Bible, and examine America's history—for what God might want to say through a relatively unknown missionary from New Zealand (now married and a US Citizen).

Finding myself drawn to the early foundations upon which this nation was built, I discovered a document that stunned me with its concise articulation of multiple world-changing truths—the Mayflower Compact of 1620. It represents the conception of what would become the United States of America. It marks a turning point in history where government begins to protect and prosper—rather than oppose and stifle—the fulfillment of God-given vision and purpose. The result was a chain reaction that kept developing these ideas throughout early America, all the way up to the birth of the United States.

I do have a message for America: In this foundational covenant, the Mayflower Compact, there are three things—powerful like dynamite, and instructive like DNA—waiting to be picked up and used to change the world again. Central to America's revival and restoration, they also speak to renewed vision and purpose for the future. We will learn what they are, where they came from, and how to take hold of them today.

America is part of a big story that has not been fully written yet. Let's come together to write the next great chapter as we see the future clearly—with *20/20 Vision for America.*

NOTES:

Figure 1. iStockPhoto.com. Used by permission.

2

Resetting the Narrative of America

The question of what to do with America's problems has seen wildly divergent answers, which range from burning the flag and rioting in the streets, all the way to prayer rallies that fill the National Mall.

A High Standard

At the moment of America's birth as a nation, exceptional ideals were held up in the Declaration of Independence. "We hold these truths to be self-evident," the founders declared, "that all men are created equal, and are endowed by their Creator with certain unalienable rights…" Yet it was clear, even then, that not everyone was treated equally.

In the following century Abraham Lincoln, and indeed the whole nation, wrestled through the tension this created—the practice of slavery versus the standard America was called to exemplify. Doubly condemning slavery, Lincoln stated, "I hate it because of the monstrous injustice of slavery itself. I hate it because it deprives our republican example of its just influence in the world."[1]

Other heroes and heroines of the past also faced this reality, and inspired us all by their response. People like Harriett Tubman and Dr. Martin Luther King, Jr. looked at the state of the nation and said, in effect, "America has fallen short of its ideals. What should we do?"

For leaders like Lincoln, Tubman and King, the answer to the problem of falling short, thankfully, has never been to abandon the ideals. Rather, the answer for them was to pray and to work, to influence and inspire, and even shed their own blood—to get closer to the ideal, to continually work toward forming *a more perfect union.*

No Time to Lose

If we are to join the great men and women of the past who called America to remember the founding principles, and to ultimately unite rather than divide—we need to do it quickly. A subversive narrative is at work in the culture. America's current imperfections and historical flaws are being used by some as a poison to induce national self-hatred, rather than a reason for repentance, reconciliation, and change. Increasingly, the narrative, "America is bad," is being broadcast into the minds of Americans, especially the young. Jesus said plainly what this leads to: "Any kingdom divided against itself is laid waste; and any city or house divided against itself will not stand" (Matthew 12:25). Unchecked, the full implication of this process will be a generation not just *ready* to trade America's foundations for another ideology—but *insisting* upon it.

What do you see when you look at America? Some see only faults, while others see only successes. Some see both and don't know what to make of it. But are these the only options for how to view America? Absolutely not.

If we are struggling to see ourselves properly, then it's time to get our vision checked.

Jesus: Eye Doctor for the Nation

An eye doctor is able to prescribe a corrective lens, allowing light to reach our eyes in such a way as to accurately represent whatever we are viewing. One well-known term used to describe accurate eyesight is "20/20 vision." As a nation, America desperately needs "20/20 vision." Right now, there is a distorted lens being pulled over the eyes of citizens through the mainstream media, much of academia, and many in the political arena. But where can we find an "eye doctor" to help a whole nation?

There is one person who is especially famous for helping people see. Jesus, we learn from the Bible, restored both natural sight and the ability to see truth. He often used stories, called parables, where the main point made important truths easier to see. One of Jesus' parables, in particular, is essential to seeing America accurately.

The Wheat and the Tares

In the "Parable of the Wheat and Tares," Jesus tells the story of a farmer who sowed good seed in his wheat field. Yet somehow, when the crop had grown, there came to be a certain type of weed (called tares) growing among the wheat. The workers who planted the seed were perplexed, wondering, "How could a good crop have anything bad in it?"

Here is the story from the book of Matthew:

> Jesus presented another parable to them, saying, "The kingdom of heaven may be compared to a man who sowed good seed in his field. But while his men were sleeping, his enemy came and sowed tares among the wheat, and went away. But when the wheat sprouted and bore grain, then the tares became evident also. The servants of the landowner came and said to him, 'Sir, did you not sow good seed in your field? How then does it have tares?' And he said to them, 'An enemy has done this!'" (Matthew 13:24-30)

Notice these two points from this story: First, the farmer is asked, "Did you not sow good seed in your field?" We know that he did. The story is explicitly describing a good crop that

Figure 1: *The "tares" described in Jesus' parable are generally considered to be "Darnel," a poisonous weed.*

was planted. Second, we learn the origin of the tares. The farmer explains to the perplexed workers, "An enemy has done this!" The point is clear that the good crop and the corruption in it are from entirely different sources.

It is also worth noting that the "tares" referred to in Jesus' parable are a weed known as "Darnel." It has some similarities in appearance to wheat (see Figure 1), but a trained eye can easily identify the difference. Darnel is both poisonous and intoxicating—a warning to be careful about the tares sown in this nation's history.

With this in mind, let's think about America. Could it be that a "good crop" was sown by God, and yet an enemy has sown "tares among the wheat?" I believe this is precisely the case. Jesus taught us to be more discerning in our evaluation of the good and bad in a situation.

Furthermore, it is at the heart of the Christian message to look at a lost, fallen, and corrupted world with eyes of redemption and restoration—seeing and calling out God's original intentions in every individual and situation. The great champions like Lincoln and King did exactly that—they had *20/20 Vision for America.* It is time to restore that vision by making a distinction between the wheat and the tares in America's past.

Toward Healing and Reconciliation

The story of the Pilgrims and the Mayflower Compact[2], I have found, are essential to seeing the "good crop" sown in what would become the United States of America. These people made it clear that they came to North America "for the glory of God and advancement of the Christian faith."[3] They viewed themselves as missionaries, with a vision of seeing the gospel of Jesus Christ thrive in the New World, and then be carried "to the remote parts of the earth."[4]

Additionally, the Mayflower Compact was a governmental covenant the passengers on the ship made before they set foot on land. It represented the beginning of the concept of

Christian self-government, where people of character could form their own civil government, and then consent to be governed by it. This was radically and wonderfully different from the model of monarchs, emperors, and tyrants. As these ideas developed in New England and elsewhere, they ultimately led to the founding of the United States of America. The world stood amazed at what grew from the good seeds that were sown.

Two final points about the good seed planted by the Pilgrims are important to note: First, their contribution to America came before the widespread breakdown of the relationship between Europeans and Native Americans. Second, the Pilgrims had nothing to do with the practice of human slavery. In other words, the good seed was sown before the tares. Seeing this allows us to go back to the beginning and know the purpose and vision that inspired these early settlers. Doing so can help us, if necessary, to reset the narrative playing in our minds concerning America's history. Far from glossing over the wrongs of the past, we must then become the agents of healing and reconciliation that are so desperately needed today.

Chapter Summary and Application

- What is the "narrative" about America playing in your mind?
- How do you deal with the fact that there are both "wheat" and "tares" in the story of America–past and present?
- Are you willing to change your view of America as you come to see the "good crop" that God planted?

NOTES:

1. John Nicolay and John Hay, *Abraham Lincoln, A History, Vol. I* (New York: The Century Co., 1909), 381.
2. The term "Pilgrims" describes the passengers on the ship *Mayflower* who came to the New World for religious liberty in 1620.
3. *Mayflower Compact*, 1620.

4. William Bradford, updated by Harold Paget, *Bradford's History of the Plymouth Settlement, 1608-1650* (New York: E. P. Dutton and Company, 1920), 21.

Figure 1. *Darnel and Wheat*, Public Domain.

3

Pulling Back the Bow

The further the bow is pulled back, the further the arrow will fly.

Imagine an ancient army going out to fight an important battle. Armed with bows and arrows, they face their enemy. When commanded to attack, they pull back the bow only a few inches and then launch. The arrows fall to the ground pathetically a few feet in front of them. Seeing an inevitable defeat, their commander rightly asks them, "What is the matter with you? Pull the bow all the way back before releasing it!"

Like the effort required to pull a bow all the way back, let me encourage you that the investment of effort to learn from history is similar. As we equip ourselves with the wisdom and insight others have labored and suffered for in centuries past, we can launch the arrows of our influence much further into the future.

In the upcoming chapters, as we move quickly over important contributions from the past—keep the analogy above in mind. The history we touch on will lead to application in the concluding chapters. It is humbling and inspiring to realize that people throughout the past were thinking of us as they laid the foundations we stand on. Learning from them, we now get to do the same for others.

The Ancient Longing for Liberty

Where did America come from? In truth, it was a long time in the making.

When Jesus walked the earth with his twelve disciples, both the Mayflower Compact and the birth of the United States of America were far in the distant future. If someone had suggested to the Jews of that time that one day, a government would be built on the idea that "all men are created equal, and endowed by their Creator with certain unalienable rights," they probably would have laughed, and ridiculed the idea.

But the Jews were looking for their own political change. Then under the thumb of the Roman Empire, they also looked back on a history of domination by Babylon, Assyria, Persia, and Greece. "When will we get to be the head again, and not the tail?" they wondered. Their hope for deliverance was in the arrival of their long-awaited Messiah.

The Jewish concept of Messiah included him being the "Son of David," the valiant military king, and like Moses, a great deliverer. They wanted deliverance from political oppression the only way the world had known it—by brute force, whether by an army or the hand of God.

For all of us, there are things about the world we wish were different. We too can be tempted to think that change can only come through force. Jesus the Messiah was about to model an entirely different form of change. His methods are as important today as they were 2000 years ago.

When Jesus began his public ministry, he knew the way his people were thinking. On one occasion when they saw him perform a miracle, the people thought they could harness his power for their own agenda. They sought to take Jesus by force and make him their King.[1]

Jesus departed from them.

Figure 1: *"The further the bow is pulled back, the further the arrow will fly."*

As it turns out, he had a different strategy.

A King Like No Other

Although Jesus resisted the petty coronation offered by the people, he was however, a king. He would soon be known as the "King of the Jews," even acknowledging it before Pontius Pilate. At this trial Jesus made an astounding comment to distinguish the nature of his kingdom from the common understanding of kings and kingdoms. He said, "My kingdom is not of this world. If My kingdom were of this world, then My servants would be fighting so that I would not be handed over to the Jews" (John 18:36). What a contrast being put on display!

Who was this king, facing condemnation to death, who would rule without taking up the sword? Rightly, Zechariah had prophesied 500 years earlier, "Behold your King is coming to you, gentle, and mounted on a donkey…" (Zechariah 9:9).

But being nothing like any king the world had known before, few recognized the immense power of how he was beginning to rule. Jesus was mocked and condemned by most of his own people. Yet within a short time after his death, resurrection, and ascension, it was said of his followers that they had "turned the world upside down."[2]

Changing the World from the Inside Out

How did Jesus, as a king, begin to transform the world?

First of all, Jesus diagnosed the root problem in the world. It was and still is the state of the human heart and mind. He made it clear that the first place change must happen is within each of us, saying, "first clean the inside of the cup and of the dish, so that the outside of it may become clean also" (Matthew 23:26).

The people of the world in Jesus' time knew all too well that a sword could stop a heart. Jesus, through his example, his teaching, and his choice to die in our place on the cross, would now demonstrate the power of love to change a heart. It has been happening ever since.

My wife and I witnessed a profound example of a man radically transformed from the inside out. Ken had been the architect working on our house plans. When we first met him, he was an unhealthy, heavy man with a very short temper. Ken was excellent at his work, but when asked to make some changes to the plans one day, he exploded, throwing our deposit check on the floor. While we managed to get the plans finished, it was a very difficult process.

A few years later, we heard Ken was in poor health and likely to die. We knew it was right to go and visit him, desiring that he find peace with God before dying. On the way to his house, familiar waves of anxiety washed over us—the same waves of anxiety we had experienced before our interactions with Ken during our house designing days. We prayed for our visit that God would soften his heart as we expressed love and forgiveness.

Ken, now thin and frail, was on a hospital bed in the same room we used to meet in. As soon as we opened the door, Ken saw us and burst into tears, asking our forgiveness for the way things had been years ago. It turned out that many others had been praying for him and talking to him about Jesus. God had done a deep work in this man's heart, transforming him into a gentle giant.

Ken recovered enough to live nine more years. We saw him in church every Sunday—a testimony to the power of inward change that Jesus spoke so much about.

A Different Kingdom

Jesus taught many things about the nature of his kingdom. It was utterly different from all the other kingdoms of the world. Jesus said that in his kingdom, the leader must be like a servant, just as he had modeled to his disciples. He taught that his kingdom was not just something to experience after death, but his disciples were to pray that his kingdom come and his will be done, on earth as it is in heaven.

Jesus described his kingdom as being like a mustard seed, one of the smallest of seeds. Yet when it grows, it becomes one of the largest plants in the garden. Although Jesus began with a small group of disciples, he was saying that his kingdom, which rules from within, would continue to grow, adding one changed heart after another. Individuals would change, and so would society, and then nations. Jesus was effectively saying, "I am going to transform the government of this world—from the inside out."

His followers and those that built the early church taught this same concept. The apostle Paul instructed, "be transformed by the renewing of your mind" (Romans 12:2). Indeed, Jesus, the King of Kings, would increasingly rule the world from within the hearts and minds of those who received him. The prophet Isaiah had described this rule of the coming Messiah more than 700 years earlier, "For a child will be born to us, a son will be given to us; And the government will rest on His shoulders...There will be no end to the increase of *His* government or of peace" (Isaiah 9:6-7).

The Roman Emperor Converts to Christianity

For the first three centuries after Jesus walked the earth, this was the basic idea of how Christianity changed the world—internal transformation comes first to each individual, leading to the external transformation of society. It was a long-term but effective strategy. So much so that it led to a significant turning point in history—the conversion of the Roman Emperor Constantine in AD 312.

Constantine's conversion resulted in a lot of good. He brought an end to the persecution of Christians that was particularly brutal in the preceding decades. Constantine convened a special meeting of bishops at a gathering now called the First Council of Nicaea in AD 325. This meeting produced the basis of the Nicene Creed, a clear statement of Christian beliefs that is still used today.

However, this period also marked the beginning of a

significant change in how Christianity would be perceived for many centuries to come. Until Constantine's conversion, Christianity had been concerned with how believers function under various governmental powers. Now, a professed Christian had the power. Imagine how strange it must have seemed—the Roman Emperor himself was now convening meetings for the church leadership!

Having a Christian emperor was uncharted territory for both the church and the state. What was to be the relationship between the two? The Mayflower Compact and the birth of the United States would bring a breakthrough on this topic, but that was more than a millennium away. Many troubled waters lay ahead.

A Gradual Return to External Force

In AD 380, Christianity officially became the state religion of the Roman Empire. By AD 800, it was the pope who crowned the emperors of the "Holy Roman Empire" in Western Europe. Over time, the Church in its institutional form became increasingly intertwined with political power and the use of force, as demonstrated by the Crusades that began in AD 1095.

As the centuries went on, even central doctrines of Christianity were at times misrepresented, in a shift of emphasis away from the inward transformation of the gospel. One example was the selling of Indulgences—money paid to the Church to purportedly reduce suffering in the afterlife, either for yourself in the future or for one of your deceased loved ones. As we will see in an upcoming chapter, this issue later sparked a call to return to the principles of Jesus' kingdom in an event known as the Reformation.

But before moving on, we should acknowledge that there have been genuine, faithful Christian men and women throughout all of church history. In spite of the issues we have mentioned, much good took place between the 4th and 14th centuries. George MacLear noted in his 1863 work *Christian*

Missions During the Middle Ages:

> The Medieval period, indeed, has been but little represented in modern accounts of Christian missions, and yet it was fertile in noble and heroic men, who laid, always in self-denial and self-sacrifice, sometimes in martyrdom and blood, the foundations of many of the Churches of modern Europe.[3]

Light on the Horizon

Having covered many centuries in a relatively short space, we will now look closer at those who shook the world around them—those whose lives were instrumental in the recovery of needed truths for both church and government. Beginning in the 14th century, these people were central to a series of profound events that would thoroughly change Europe, forging ideas that would ultimately help shape America.

Get ready to "pull back your bow."

Chapter Summary and Application

- Why did Jesus, with all power at his command, choose to transform the world from the inside out?
- Are there ways you have tried to change your own behavior without letting God change your heart and mind first?
- As you consider the things you want to see change in the world, what is your approach? Do you have a long-term strategy for transforming hearts and minds?

NOTES:

1. John 6:14-15
2. Acts 17:6
3. George MacLear, *A History of Christian Missions During the Middle Ages* (Cambridge and London: MacMillan and Co., 1863), vi.

Figure 1. Creative Commons CC0. Public Domain.

4

In the Beginning Was the Word

> In the beginning was the Word, and the Word was with God, and the Word was God. He was in the beginning with God. All things came into being through Him, and apart from Him nothing came into being that has come into being. (John 1:1-3)

God began everything with the Word.

The heavens and the earth, all life and mankind, the nation of Israel and the foretelling of the Messiah—all these and more began with the Word.

Jesus, when tempted by the devil before beginning his ministry, refuted every deception of Satan with a reference to Scripture, saying, "It is written…"

It should come as no surprise then that access to the Bible has been resisted over the centuries by extreme spiritual hostility. At the same time, when made available in a people's mother tongue, astonishing results have followed.

A fierce battle raged over translation of the Bible into English. The battle was eventually won, creating an epicenter of influence—influence that spread to the four corners of the earth through the English language.

Here is a little of this epic story.

Trapped in an Unspoken Language

Increased access to the Bible had produced major change in Europe by the time the Pilgrims sailed to North America in 1620. In particular, the Bible had been the principal book of reference for leaders of the Reformation, a period of great change that ran from 1517 to 1648 (and which we will examine in greater detail in later chapters). The Reformers' study and application of biblical concepts changed thinking about the church, education, government, and more. But why was Bible access such a big problem, and how did that change?

Around AD 405, a new translation of the Bible in Latin was completed. Known today as the "Latin Vulgate," this translation (mostly by St. Jerome) became the church's official Bible for more than 1000 years. The problem was that Latin eventually faded from use as a spoken language, while remaining the language of the church and the Scriptures.

Making things worse, the church came to believe common people should never read and interpret a Bible in their mother tongue. In 1229, this became official church law at the Council of Toulouse. It was pronounced that laypeople should not have the Old or New Testament even in Latin, and more strictly condemned the possession of Scripture translated into the common languages of the day.

A Lesson from Pentecost

In the 14th century, a breakthrough came in the battle to get Scripture into everyday language. It came through John Wycliffe, an English scholar, theologian, and professor at Oxford University. Wycliffe was an outstanding intellect. He was described by one of his contemporaries as "unrivaled" in philosophy, debate, and other scholastic exercises.[1] He would need all the strength he could muster, both mental and spiritual, for the conflict he faced.

To Wycliffe, the need for Scripture in the peoples' common

Figure 1: *John Wycliffe was a powerful influencer, depicted here sending out his disciples equipped with Scripture in English*

language was fundamental. He pointed out that God had given this understanding to the early church at the outpouring of the Holy Spirit at Pentecost. Acts 2 records this account, where those touched by the Holy Spirit were heard speaking many different languages. Those visiting Jerusalem from around the world were amazed and astonished, saying, "We hear them in our *own* tongues speaking of the mighty deeds of God" (Acts 2:11).

"Christ and his apostles," Wycliffe asserted, "converted the most part of the world by making known the Scripture in a language which was most familiar to the people."[2] Turning his convictions into action, John Wycliffe oversaw the translation of the Bible into Middle English.[3]

Ferocious Opposition

In addition to advocating for Scripture translation, Wycliffe was a reformer at heart. He wrote extensively on the reforms he believed were needed in the church. Between this and his translation work, he summoned the full wrath of the church hierarchy.

To get a feel for the firestorm he created, it is worth quoting the following response he issued to those condemning his work. In it, we see the formidable Wycliffe who changed the course of history:

> You say...that it is heresy to speak of the Holy Scriptures in English. You call me a heretic because I have translated the Bible into the common tongue of the people. Do you know whom you blaspheme? Did not the Holy Ghost give the Word of God at first in the mother tongue of the nations to whom it was addressed? Why do you speak against the Holy Ghost? You say that the Church of God is in danger from this book. How can that be? Is it not from the Bible only that we learn that God set up such a society as a Church on the earth? Is it not the Bible that gives all her authority to the Church? Is it not from the Bible that we learn who is the Builder and Sovereign of the Church, what are the laws by which she is to be governed, and the rights and privileges of her members? Without the Bible what charter has the church to show for all these? It is you who place the Church in jeopardy by hiding [the Scriptures].[4]

Despite strong denouncements from the church, Wycliffe had support from loyal followers, as well as certain academic and political circles. As he held his ground on the importance of Scripture translation, his example, passion, and determination blazed a trail many others would follow.

With good reason, Wycliffe's name today is synonymous with Bible translation worldwide.

The True Price of Your Bible

The next time you grab some coffee, curl up in your favorite chair, and open your Bible, consider for a moment the significance of the book you hold. The English Bible represents a victory in one of the great battles of the ages. It seems as though dark forces could foresee the light that would

In ye bigynnyng was ye word & ye word was
at god & god was ye word yis was in ye bigy
nnyng at god alle yingis weren maad bi hym:
and wiyouten hym was maad noying yat ying
yat was maad in hym was lyf and ye lyf was
ye lizt of men/ and lizt schyneþ in derknessis and
derknessis comprehendiden not it/

Figure 2: *A page from John Wycliffe's translation into Middle English, showing John 1:1-5.*

break forth in the world if this translation ever succeeded.

They were right about that.

The trail of history we are following will show that there would be no United States of America if this mission had failed.

Where Wycliffe established a beachhead in the battle for the English Bible, a man named William Tyndale would help win the war—and in so doing, pay the ultimate price.

William Tyndale

Tyndale studied at Oxford in the early 16th century. As a gifted linguist, he became fluent in at least eight languages and was intent on translating the Bible. He is famously reported to have encountered a scholar who claimed, "We were better to be without God's law than the Pope's." Tyndale responded to the scholar, "If God spare my life, before many years I will cause a boy who drives a plough, to know more of the Scripture than you do."[5]

Tyndale's life was spared long enough to produce a new translation of the Bible in more modern English. But before fully completing the project, he was betrayed to authorities for his illegal work. After imprisonment, Tyndale's execution came in 1536. His last words prior to being strangled and burned at the stake were a loud and fervent prayer, "Lord! Open the King of England's eyes!"[6]

Shortly after Tyndale's death, Henry VIII authorized the printing of the "Great Bible" based on Tyndale's translation, placing it in all the churches of England. The tide had now turned in favor of the most influential book in history being widely accessible in English.

Tyndale's work influenced every subsequent English translation. He helped enrich the English language itself, giving us many phrases still used today, such as "the salt of the earth" and "the powers that be."

Wycliffe's Legacy and its Effect on America

John Wycliffe was hated by many to the degree that he altered the course of history through Bible translation.

The Archbishop of Canterbury described Wycliffe after his death as "that pestilent wretch of damnable memory, John Wycliffe, son of the old serpent, yea, the forerunner and disciple of Anti-Christ...He, as the complement of his wickedness, invented a new translation of the Scriptures into his mother tongue."[7]

Four decades after his death, the Pope ordered that Wycliffe's bones be exhumed and burned, and the ashes cast into the Swift river. This act was unintentionally prophetic. As surely as the Swift river made its way to the Atlantic Ocean and beyond, so too would the influence of the Bible in English. As historian Thomas Fuller put it, "the ashes of Wycliffe are the emblem of his doctrine which now is dispersed all the world over."[8]

Nobody could have imagined the impact that translation of the Bible into English would have on the world. The Bible was like a seed planted into the English language—producing the fruit of worldwide influence. English itself would grow from a relatively obscure, localized language, to become a leading means of international communication. Influential Englishmen, like William Blackstone on the subject of law and John Locke on government, have changed the world through their written works, which were derived from concepts in the Bible.

It seems that when the Bible is honored in a nation, God gives that nation a place of honor—as the Scripture says, "Those who honor Me, I will honor, and those who despise Me will be lightly esteemed" (1 Samuel 2:30).

The Pilgrims, though few in number, honored God and his Word. They too have been honored with a special place in America's history.

Chapter Summary and Application

- Are you winning the battle in your own life? Is anything working to keep you from reading and understanding the Bible?
- If you've never read the Bible all the way through, consider making it your goal to read the entire Bible in the next twelve months.
- How can you share the Bible with others who do not yet have a copy, such as immigrants and foreign students studying in America?

NOTES:

1. Robert Vaughan, *The Life and Opinions of John de Wycliffe, Vol. I* (London: B.J. Holdsworth, Hatchard and Son, 1828), 233-234.
2. Robert Vaughan, *Tracts and Treatises of John Wycliffe* (London: Blackburn and Pardon, 1845), lxiii.

3. *Middle English* describes form of the English language from *c.* 1150 to *c.* 1470.
4. James Wylie, *The History of Protestantism* (New York, Paris, London, and Melbourne: Cassell and Company, Limited, 1899), 113.
5. John Foxe, *The Acts and Monuments of John Foxe: A New and Complete Edition, Vol. V* (London: R. B. Seely and W. Burnside, 1838), 117.
6. Ibid, 127.
7. Thomas Boultbee, *A History of the Church of England* (London, Longmans, Green, and Co., 1879), 320-321.
8. Thomas Fuller, *The Church History of Britain, Vol. I* (London: Thomas Tegg, 1842), 493.

Figure 1. William Frederick Yeames, *Wyclif Giving "The Poor Priests" His Translation of the Bible,* Public Domain.
Figure 2. *Wycliffe Bible,* Public Domain.

5

The Power of the Press

I wisdom dwell with prudence, and find out knowledge of witty inventions. (Proverbs 8:12)

He was financially unsuccessful. He was sued and lost his business. But one thing Johannes Gutenberg did not do was quit. He persevered and the result was an invention that changed the world.

In order to fulfill Wycliffe's vision of getting a Bible into everyone's hands, translation of Scripture was just the beginning. A much faster method of duplication was the next great challenge—and the solution could not come soon enough.

Let's Hear it for the Monks!

We owe a debt of gratitude to those who have reproduced the Bible's manuscripts throughout history. For many centuries, this work was done by monks. The early Christian monastic movement emphasized literacy, and later, the work of hand duplicating texts. A special room, a *scriptorium*, was set aside in the monastery for this long and taxing work. An early leader of the monastic text-copying movement was the Roman statesman Cassiodorus, who lived in the 6th century. During his retirement, he founded a monastery where he commissioned monks to copy sacred texts. Cassiodorus describes the arduous task with passion:

> With his fingers he gives life to men, and arms them against the wiles of the devil...What he writes in his cell will be scattered far and wide over distant Provinces. Man multiplies the heavenly words...the three fingers of his hand express the utterances of the Holy Trinity. The fast-travelling reed writes down the holy words and thus avenges the malice of the Wicked One who caused a reed to be used to smite the head of the Saviour.[1]

How long would it take to hand copy a Bible? To get some perspective, an English Bible has around 780,000 words. If you were capable of writing ten words per minute with ink and quill, wrote for eight full hours per day, and took a Sabbath rest each week, the task would take 190 days! As you probably suspect, in reality, it would take much longer. The process would also involve reviewing source material, checking your own work, and the constant need to get up and stretch. A scribe from the tenth century, Prior Petrus of the San Domingo de Silos monastery in Spain, described the copyist's task as one that produced dimmed eyesight, an aching hunched back and the knitting together of the chest to the stomach.[2]

A Revolution Begins

Thankfully, the speed at which Scripture could be reproduced went to a whole new level when Gutenberg, the son of a German goldsmith, invented a new kind of movable-type printing press in the 1400s. The day was near when great numbers of people would not only understand the language of the Bible, but have their own copy as well! As we have seen, up until this time, copying major texts such as the Bible was painfully slow. Gutenberg's invention began the revolution of greater duplication speed, availability, and affordability of

***Figure 1:** A Medieval monk copying a manuscript by hand.*

printed material.

The printing press began to greatly reduce the cost of large literary works. For example, in the 13th century the price of a Bible "was equal to the entire wages in money of a laboring man for over fifteen years,"[3] according to an American Bible Society source. By the 16th century, Bibles such as Martin Luther's German translation were affordable to the working person, as we shall soon see.

Perhaps it should not surprise us that the world's most produced book, the Bible, was the first full-sized work printed on Gutenberg's press. Sometimes referred to as the 42-line Bible—distinguishing it from a subsequent edition with 36 lines of text per column—the original Gutenberg Bible is today one of the most valuable books in the world. Approximately 180 copies were made. Although printed in Latin, this iconic work paved the way for the Bible to be printed in a growing number of languages, a trend that is still increasing today.

Perfect Timing

With mass production of the Bible now emerging, motivation to get one and read it was about to skyrocket. The reason would be the Great Reformation, the next major event we will look at. The leading figure in this period was a previously little-known German monk and scholar named Martin Luther. He saw the untapped potential of the printing press for communicating his message of reform.

It has been said that the power of the press belongs to those who own one. Luther, understanding this, recruited highly skilled printers and illustrators to thoroughly leverage the technology of his day, quickly becoming the most published author in Europe.

Fascinating records have been preserved that give insight into how Luther and the Reformation led to a rapid expansion of literature in Germany:

- In the five years preceding the Reformation (1513-1517), a total of just 527 titles were published.[4]

gentes: incipientibus ab iherosolima.
Vos aũt testes estis horũ. Et ego mit-
tam promissum patris mei i vos: vos
aũt sedete in civitate. quoadusq; indu-
amini virtute ex alto. Eduxit aũt eos
foras in bethaniam: ⁊ elevatis mani-
bus suis benedixit eis. Et factũ est dũ
benediceret illis recessit ab eis: ⁊ fereba-
tur in celum. Et ipsi adorantes regres-
si sunt in iherusalem cum gaudio ma-
gno: et erant semper in templo lau-
dantes et benedicentes deum amen.
Explicit euangeliũ sc̃dm lucã. Incip p̃lo-
gus i euangeliũ sc̃dm iohannẽ.

Hic est iohannes euange-
lista un9 ex discipulis dñi:
qui virgo a deo electus ẽ:
quẽ de nuptijs volentem
nubere vocavit deus. Cui virginitatis
in hoc duplex testimoniũ datur in euangelio: q et pre ceteris dilectus a deo
dicit: et huic matrem suã de cruce com-
mendavit dñs. ut virginẽ virgo serva-
ret. Deniq; manifestans in euangelio
q erat ipse incorruptibilis verbi opus
inchoans. solus verbũ carnẽ factum
esse. nec lumen a tenebris cõprehensũ
fuisse testatur: primũ signũ ponẽs qd
in nuptijs fecit dñs ostendens q ipse
erat: ut legentibus demonstraret q ubi
dñs invitatus sit deficere nuptiarũ vi-
num debeat: et veteribus immutatis.
nova omnia que a cristo instituuntur
appareãt. Hoc aũt euãgeliũ scripsit in
asia. postea q̃ i pathmos insula apo-
calipsim scripserat: ut cui i principio ca-
nonis incorruptibile principiũ p̃notatur
in genesi: ei etiã incorruptibilis finis
p virginẽ i apocalipsi redderet dicẽte
cristo ego sum alpha et o. Et hic ẽ iohannes: qui sciens supervenisse diem re-
cessus sui. Convocatis discipulis suis
in epheso. per multa signorũ experimen-
ta p̃mens cristũ descendens i defossũ
sepulture sue locũ facta oratione. po-
situs est ad patres suos: tam extrane9
a dolore mortis q̃ a corruptione carnis invenitur alienus. Tamen post o-
mnes euãgeliũ scripsit: ⁊ hoc virgini
debebatur. Quorũ tamẽ vel scriptorũ tẽpo-
ris disposicio. vel librorũ ordinatio ideo
a nobis per singula non exponitur:
ut sciendi desiderio collato et querẽti-
bus fructus laboris: ⁊ deo magiste-
rij doctrina servetur. Explicit p̃log9.
Incipit euangeliũ sc̃dm iohannẽ.

In principio erat verbũ: ⁊ verbũ erat
apud deũ: et de9 erat verbũ. Hoc erat
in principio apud deũ. Omnia p ipsm
facta sunt: ⁊ sine ipso factum est nichil.
Quod factũ est in ipso vita erat: ⁊ vita
erat lux hominũ: et lux in tenebris lu-
cet. ⁊ tenebre eã nõ comp̃henderũt. Fu-
it homo missus a deo: cui nomẽ erat io-
hãnes. Hic venit i testimoniũ ut testimoniũ p̃hiberet de lumine: ut omnes
crederent p illũ. Nõ erat ille lux: sed ut
testimoniũ p̃hiberet de lumine. Erat
lux vera: que illuminat omnẽ homi-
nem venientem in hũc mundũ. In mũ-
do erat: ⁊ mũdus p ipsm factus est: et
mũdus eũ non cognovit. In p̃pria venit: ⁊ sui eũ nõ receperũt. Quotquot aũt
receperũt eũ. dedit eis potestatem filios
dei fieri: hijs qui credũt in nomine ei9.
Qui nõ ex sanguinibus neq; ex voluntate carnis. neq; ex voluntate viri: sed
ex deo nati sunt. Et verbũ caro factum
est: et habitavit in nobis. Et vidimus
gloriã ei9. gloriam quasi unigeniti a
patre: plenũ gratie ⁊ veritatis. Johannes testimonium p̃hibet de ipso. ⁊ cla-
mat dicens. Hic erat quẽ dixi: q post
me venturus est. ante me factus est:

Figure 2: *A page from the "Gutenberg Bible," often called the 42-line Bible after the number of lines in each column.*

- In the first six years of the Reformation, that number rose to 3113 titles.[5]
- In 1523, four-fifths of published titles were in support of the Reformation.[6]

At that time, Martin Luther himself far outsold any other author, one of whom—Erasmus of Rotterdam—complained that "the people would read and buy no other books than Luther's."[7]

The Bible in German

Luther's many publications pointed readers to the Bible as the source of authority in matters relating to the Christian faith and its application to society. To complement this, he translated and published the Bible in German, with an emphasis on using the common language of the day. This effort made Luther's Bible the German people's Bible, to the point that it even helped shape the German language.

Beginning with his New Testament published in 1522 (followed by the Old Testament in 1534), Luther's Bible sold in great numbers. The first edition of his New Testament sold 5000 copies in less than three months.[8] The main printer used by Luther, Hans Lufft, printed over 100,000 copies of his Bible, in addition to the editions of other printers.[9] In the words of historian Philip Schaff, "The precious little volume, which contains the wisdom of the whole world, made its way with lightning speed into the palaces of princes, the castles of knights, the convents of monks, the studies of priests, the houses of citizens, the huts of peasants."[10]

Technology Changed the World

Not everyone was excited about the rapid increase in printed literature. For example, in Gutenberg's hometown of Mainz, where he invented the printing press, the Archbishop issued a prohibition in 1486 on the sale of all German translations of Greek and Latin works not authorized by the church. The banning and burning of books was not uncommon in the wake of Gutenberg's invention. But in spite of official lists of banned books, such as the church's *Index Librorum prohibitorum,* the printing press prevailed in bringing about greater access to the Bible and other important literature.

Johannes Gutenberg's invention changed the world. Multiplication of the Bible through cutting-edge technology was inseparable from the reforming of Europe, which helped equip the Pilgrims with the truth and understanding they carried across the Atlantic.

Gutenberg persevered in his quest to transform printing—and we have been blessed by his contribution to the ideas that influenced America. As we stand on the shoulders of those before us, let's persevere in our quest to preserve America's blessing for future generations.

Chapter Summary and Application

- Will you persevere in developing your practical giftings and abilities–devoting them to the purposes of God?
- What is the "Gutenberg Press" of the 21st Century?
- In what ways can you better utilize the technology of today to reach out to those around you, and those far away?

NOTES:

1. Thomas Hodgkin, *The Letters of Cassiodorus* (London: Henry Frowde, 1886), 58.
2. Irina Metzler, *Disability in Medieval Europe: Thinking about Physical Impairment in the High Middle Ages, c.1100–c.1400* (London and New York: Routledge, Taylor and Francis Group, 2006).
3. *The Manual of the American Bible Society* (New York: American Bible Society Press, 1893), 45.
4. Philip Schaff, *History of the Christian Church, Vol. VI* (New York, Charles Scribner's Sons, 1888), 560-561.
5. Ibid.
6. Ibid, 561.
7. Ibid, 561.
8. Ibid, 561.
9. Ibid, 561-562.

10. Ibid, 564.
Figure 1. *Medieval Monk,* Public Domain.
Figure 2. *Gutenberg Bible,* Public Domain.

6

World Changers

Yet once more I will shake not only the earth, but also the heaven…so that those things which cannot be shaken may remain. (Hebrews 12:26-27)

It was like an earthquake.

The convergence of courage and conviction, of Bible translation and printing press, shook the institutions of church and government. People and ideas were shaken. Eyes were opened. Europe and the world would be forever changed by the period that began in 1517—the Great Reformation.

Ripples That Reached Across the Atlantic

When the Pilgrims set sail for the New World in 1620, it had been 103 years since the Reformation began. Its principal leaders and their ideas were towering influences in the Pilgrims' minds, significantly shaping their views on church and government.

As a major link in the chain of events we are following, the Reformation contributed to the powerful ideas in the Mayflower Compact, which in turn helped forge America.

How it Began

As highlighted in previous chapters, over time, the Church drifted from the message Jesus had given his disciples, and from the teachings of the early church recorded in the New Testament. This drift produced the state of the church prior to the Reformation.

All too often wielding its influence through force and coercion, rather than the inward transformation and renewal of the gospel, there was a need for reform in various aspects of the church. For example, the authority of Scripture—which Jesus many times affirmed—was clearly being superseded by certain traditions of the church.

It was one of these traditions, taken to the extreme, that sparked the beginning of the Reformation. That tradition was known as the sale of "indulgences."

The church had developed the concept of an indulgence as a way someone could reduce the punishment due for their sins. In order to obtain an indulgence, the church required certain actions or good works be performed. However, the Bible plainly says, "By grace you have been saved through faith; and that not of yourselves, it is the gift of God" (Ephesians 2:8).

Indulgences for Sale

Eventually, payment of money to the church became one of the "good works" for securing an indulgence. Packaging God's mercy as a marketable product would prove to be a provocative action. It would stir one man in particular with a righteous indignation—the kind that stirred Jesus when he saw the temple filled with dishonest financial dealings rather than the business of his kingdom. Jesus said, "Is it not written, 'My house shall be called a house of prayer for all the nations'? but you have made it a robbers' den" (Mark 11:17).

The abuse of indulgences reached its height in 1517, when the church wanted to rebuild St. Peter's Basilica in Rome. In Germany, the Grand Commissioner for indulgences was Yohann Tetzel. Intent on raising the most money possible

Figure 1: *"The soul flies out of purgatory as soon as the money thrown into the chest rattles," proclaimed Yohann Tetzel as he sold "indulgences."*

through indulgences, he began preaching the idea that "the soul flies out of purgatory as soon as the money thrown into the chest rattles."[1]

Tetzel was brazen in his methods. He sent example sermons to local clergymen to help them prepare their people to buy indulgences, which ended up stoking the fires of reformation further. One of these sermons reads, in part:

> "How many mortal sins are committed in a day, how many in a week, how many in a month, how many in a year, how many in the whole extent of life! They are well-nigh numberless, and those that commit them must needs suffer endless punishment in the burning pains of Purgatory. But with these confessional letters you will be able, at any time in life, to obtain full indulgence for all penalties imposed upon you..."[2]

Martin Luther

In 1483, Martin Luther came into the world, seemingly born

for "such a time as this." Wycliffe and Gutenberg had set the stage for truly dramatic change, and Luther would now take the lead role.

Initially studying law following his father's wishes, Luther quickly abandoned this pursuit in favor of philosophy and theology. He had a deep concern for finding truth, as well as certainty in his relationship with God. After nearly being struck by lightning in a storm in 1505, a terrified Luther vowed to become a monk, and he did so promptly. He joined a monastic order that same year and was ordained two years later, in 1507.

During his time at St. Augustine's monastery in Erfurt, Germany, Luther experienced the despair of trying to pursue a right relationship with God through a focus on works of penance and self-denial. This was in part the result of an unfortunate translation choice in the Latin Vulgate.

Instead of translating the Greek word for *repent* in its primary meaning "to change one's mind or purpose," the Vulgate used the Latin word "pœnitentiae," meaning *penance.* This meant that readers of the Latin Bible—for more than a thousand years—had heard John the Baptist, Jesus, the disciples, Peter, and the apostle Paul preaching a gospel declaring, "Pœnitentiam agite!" This phrase was understood as "Do penance!" No wonder there was such an emphasis on works of penance in the church during that period.

The 2003 movie "Luther"[3] powerfully captures the concept of Luther's disillusionment, as he seeks to get closer to God by climbing, on his knees, the steps of the *Scala Sancta,* the "Holy Stairs" in Rome. Luther is depicted as an earnest monk—yet with growing doubts that penance and indulgences are going to help him or others.

The Truth Shall Set You Free

Luther's journey from despair to transformation was helped along by some timely counsel. A key figure in Luther's life was Johann von Staupitz, his superior in the monastic order. It was Staupitz who pointed Luther's focus away from penance and self-effort, and instead to Jesus and His provision of a righteousness obtained through faith. Luther said later in life that if God had not helped him through Staupitz, "I would have long ago sunk to Hell."[4]

Luther describes the heart of his transformation this way:

> "At length, by the mercy of God, meditating days and nights, I observed the connection of the words, namely, 'Therein is the righteousness of God revealed from faith to faith, as it is written, The just shall live by faith.' Here I felt myself absolutely born again; the gates of heaven were opened, and I had entered paradise itself."[5]

For Luther, a vigorous scholar who obtained his Doctor of Theology and served as Chair of Theology at Wittenberg University, this discovery of a living faith coupled with his knowledge of the Scripture produced the conviction that aspects of the Church needed drastic reform. He had experienced a profound internal change. Now, the world around him would change too.

The Famous 95 Theses

On October 31, 1517, Martin Luther nailed his "95 Theses" to the door of Castle Church in Wittenberg, Germany—in response to the church's corruption of selling indulgences. This was a customary practice for academics of that time, by which they shared ideas intended for scholarly discussion.

A look at some of Luther's 95 Theses gives a feel for the Reformer he was, and the issue he was addressing:

i. They preach man, who say that the soul flies out of purgatory as soon as the money thrown into the chest rattles.

ii. It is certain that, when the money rattles in the chest, avarice and gain may be increased, but the suffrage of the Church depends on the will of God alone.

iii. Every Christian who feels true compunction has of right plenary remission of pain and guilt, even without letters of pardon.

iv. Those who believe that, through letters of pardon, they are made sure of their own salvation, will be eternally damned along with their teachers.[6]

Figure 2: *An artist's impression of Martin Luther after nailing his 95 Theses on the Castle Church door in 1517.*

When the 95 Theses were posted, not only did the scholarly take notice, everyday people did too. They were interested in what Luther had to say on indulgences, and later, on the wide range of topics he addressed. As the printing press spread his popular writings far and wide, a major turning point in history was underway.

Refusal to Recant

Luther's messages stirred up a hornet's nest of opposition. In 1521, the Holy Roman Emperor Charles V tried him as a heretic. He was asked to recant what he had written. He did not—but he did apologize for the harsh tone used in some of his writings. Luther chose to hold fast to the main points he

Figure 3: *Martin Luther on trial at the "Diet of Worms." The diet (assembly) was held in Worms, Germany.*

had made, famously saying at his trial:

> "Unless I am convinced by witness of Scripture or plain reason—for I do not believe in the Pope or in Councils alone since it is agreed that they have often erred and contradicted themselves—I am overcome by the Scriptures which I have adduced and my conscience is caught in the word of God. I neither can nor will recant anything, for it is neither safe nor right to act against one's conscience...God help me, Amen."[7]

Martin Luther was a man of tremendous courage! He had his flaws as well. His manner was blunt and crude at times, and his later writings concerning the Jews were utterly unacceptable. Nevertheless, along with others, Luther and the Reformation set changes in motion that would transform Europe and strongly influence the founding of America.

What were these changes? They were first of all changes in the way people thought about the structure and practice of the Church, but it would not stop there. Let's look at some main points of the Reformation and how their influence reached beyond the Church.

Point One: Justification by Faith

As mentioned, the phrase from Romans 1:17, "The righteous shall live by faith," was central to Luther's transformation. When he realized that Jesus' sacrifice on the cross—not his own works—was the source of his righteousness before God, Luther was truly "born again."

This renewed emphasis on genuine, saving faith was essential in its own right. It was also an essential step toward changes in the realm of government that would develop in the following centuries. A vital aspect of the Christian message is that Christ "dwells in our hearts through faith" (Ephesians 3:17), and that "where the Spirit of the Lord is, there is liberty" (2 Corinthians 3:17).

Before liberty at the level of civil government can succeed in a nation, there needs to be liberty at the individual level. So we see that the Reformation helped prepare the way for the concept of self-government, which the Mayflower Compact modeled.

Point Two: The Priesthood of All Believers

Luther emphasized the privilege and responsibility of all believers to have direct access to the presence of God, read and interpret the Bible, and then teach and instruct others. These things are not, he argued, the exclusive privilege of formally trained church leaders.

Luther was not dismissing the necessity of structure within the Church. He was reminding the world of the central message of Christianity—that Jesus died and was raised to life so everyone can have access to God's presence regardless of wealth, education, power, or position.

> "Through baptism all of us are consecrated to the priesthood, as St Peter says in I Peter ii, 'Ye are a royal priesthood, a priestly kingdom,' and the book of Revelation

says, "Thou hast made us by Thy blood to be priests and kings."[8]

This idea of the priesthood of all believers led to a rapid expansion of Christianity. It did so by empowering and commissioning the individual to step up to his or her responsibility before God. People began to see more clearly their value and place of participation, which had not previously been allowed, much less encouraged. Things that had been only allowed for the clergy, like reading and interpreting the Scripture, were now being practiced by laypeople.

Changing views on church government naturally led to rethinking the structure of civil government. Most prominent among the emergence of new forms of church government, were the Presbyterian and Congregational models. Congregational churches in particular emphasize having the governing authority at the local level rather than at the top of a distant hierarchy.

The Pilgrims, who had already adopted the Congregational model for their church, adapted this concept when they drafted the Mayflower Compact. They placed authority for civil government at the local level also. This was a radical departure from being governed by a king, emperor, or tyrant, and a major step toward a government "of the people, by the people, and for the people."[9]

Point Three: Authority of Scripture

Luther insisted that the Bible is the highest source of authority for the church on a matter, rather than the opinions of the church's leaders, its traditions or its legal decisions. This concept is commonly referred to by its Latin name, *Sola Scriptura.* In particular, Luther contested the idea that the pope alone had final authority to interpret the Bible.

Luther had experienced the power of the Word of God after searching it intently himself. As we saw, it was a phrase of Scripture that brought Luther to a life-filled relationship with God. He and the other leading Reformers such as John

Calvin, were intimately acquainted with the Bible.

"I have now for some time," said Luther, "read the Bible twice through every year. It is a great tree, and all its words are twigs and branches, and every twig and spray I have struck to find out what was on it, and what it was good for; yet, knock as often as I will, down comes a fresh handful of fruit."[10]

John Calvin said, "As by the rising of the sun darkness is put to flight, and all things appear distinctly to the view, so also when God comes forth with the teaching of his word, all the deceptions of Satan must necessarily be dissipated."[11]

Jesus constantly referred to the authority of Scripture, and so did the reformers. It is a hallmark of every great work of God.

Reform Spreads

Through the Reformation, powerful winds of change began to blow. These winds would soon blow throughout England and be caught by the sails of the Mayflower, carrying the seeds of change to the New World.

Chapter Summary and Application

- Before Luther changed the world, he himself was transformed. Have you set apart a season of your life to diligently seek God like Luther did?
- How important was knowledge of the Bible to the Reformation?
- Is it possible to stand for truth without being harsh or crude?

NOTES:

1. Martin Luther, *First Principles of the Reformation: Or, The Ninety-five Theses and the Three Primary Works of Luther Translated Into English* (London: John Murray, 1883), 8 (97).
2. Johann Tetzel, "Extract from Sermon Given by Tetzel to Parochial Clergy as Pattern for Indulgence Preaching," in *Translations and Reprints from the Original Sources of European History: Reformation Number, Vols. 1 - 6*

(The Department of History of the University of Pennsylvania: 1897), 4-5 (34-35).
3. *Luther*, directed by Eric Till (R.S. Entertainment Inc., 2003).
4. *American Lutheran Survey, Vol I* (Columbia, South Carolina: Lutheran Survey Publishing Company, 1914), 38.
5. Martin Luther, *Luther's Primary Works, Together with his Shorter and Larger Catechisms* (London: Hodder and Stoughton, 1896), 430.
6. Martin Luther, *First Principles of the Reformation, or, The Ninety-five Theses and the Three Primary Works of Dr. Martin Luther, Translated into English,* (London: John Murray, 1883), *6-9 (95-98).*
7. Charles Beard, *Martin Luther and the Reformation in Germany Until the Close of the Diet of Worms* (London: Philip Green, 1896), 441.
8. Martin Luther, *Works of Martin Luther, With Introductions and Notes, Vol. II* (Philadelphia: A. J. Holman Company and The Castle Press, 1915), 66.
9. Abraham Lincoln, *Gettysburg Address*, November 19, 1863.
10. *The Lutheran Pioneer, Volume 30* (Evangelical Lutheran Synodical Conference of North America, 1908), 85.
11. John Calvin, *Commentaries on the Twelve Minor Prophets, Vol. V* (Edinburgh: The Calvin Translation Society, 1849), 378.

Figure 1. *The Sale of Absolutions,* Public Domain.
Figure 2. *Martin Luther's Theses,* Ferdinand Wilhelm Pauwels, Public Domain.
Figure 3. *Luther at the Diet of Worms*, Anton von Werner, Public Domain.

7

Against All Odds

"Run! Take cover!" my wife recalls hearing in war-torn South Sudan, while her relief team waited for their flat tire to be fixed. The sight of enemy bombers overhead added distress to the extreme frustration they were experiencing because of delays. They had just two weeks to get supplies to many villages suffering from their nation's civil war. A day later, however, they learned that twenty-four bombs had been dropped on the exact location they would have been in, if the flat tire had not happened. The team's time of "trial" resulted in their preservation and the fulfillment of their mission to help many others.

Trials that Turned to Gold

It is often difficult to recognize these times—when something good is being forged in the midst of adversity. The decades leading up to the Pilgrims' departure for America were like that. While seeking to implement Reformation ideals in the church of England, many Christians faced persecution. But with hindsight, we can see the stage was being set for something spectacular on the other side of the Atlantic.

The Exodus

Out of England and into New England they flowed—a stream of people with strong Christian faith, character and resolve—driven along by religious persecution. Without a concentration of people in New England who possessed these qualities, there could never have been the development of liberty that America came to be known for.

This great exodus from England of those seeking religious freedom is a big part of America's story. The way the Reformation affected England helps to explain why it happened. So, tighten your seatbelt for just a few minutes, as we quickly look over how important aspects of America were being forged in the furnace of England's Reformation.

Henry VIII Gets Miffed

The influence of the Reformation, begun in Germany, swept into England during the reign of King Henry VIII (1509 - 1547). Because of England's formal alignment with the Roman Catholic Church since AD 597, Henry initially resisted and even persecuted supporters of the movement. These so-called "Protestants" were seen as protesting against the Catholic Church.

Henry's views changed when his will was crossed by the Pope. He wanted to annul his marriage to Catherine of Aragon, who had not given him a son as heir. His desire was to marry Anne Boleyn, a maid of honor in the royal court with whom he had been infatuated. Only the Pope could grant the permission Henry wanted, but Pope Clement VII refused to give it.

In reaction, Henry broke with the Roman Catholic Church and established the Church of England in its place, a process that began in 1532. Through the "Act of Supremacy" passed by parliament in 1534, Henry was free from the Pope's control, having appointed himself as "the only Supreme Head in Earth

Figure 1: *Persecution in England brought about a wave of migration to the New World.*

of the Church of England."[1]

Henry made England an outwardly Protestant nation, but his power-driven departure from the Catholic Church represented nothing of the heart of the Reformation. Grass-roots reformers in England still faced persecution if they opposed the King's views. Nevertheless, he fueled the fire of true reform by authorizing the printing of "The Great Bible" and requiring its placement in every church in England. An estimated 20,000 copies were distributed.[2]

The Nine-Year-Old King

Henry VIII died in 1547, bringing nine-year-old Edward VI (1547 - 1553) to the throne. Under this young and malleable King, the Archbishop of Canterbury, Thomas Cranmer, used his influence to make meaningful changes not possible under Henry VIII. Most notably, his famous *Book of Common Prayer* (revised and still in use today) provided a format for church services in English rather than Latin. He also brought reform to the policy of priests having to be celibate, and allowed them to marry.

Bloody Mary

But this tide of favor for Protestant reform turned when Edward died in 1553 at age 15. A new wave of persecution arrived in the form of Queen Mary I, later referred to as "Bloody Mary." Mary resolved to undo the advances of the English Reformation and restore England's position under the Roman Catholic Church. Using the legal authority of the revived "Heresy Acts,"[3] numerous Protestants were executed, and many more fled England to escape persecution. Hundreds were burned at the stake, including Thomas Cranmer.

Elizabeth – Pray or Pay

The death of Bloody Mary in 1558 brought another reversal as Queen Elizabeth I took the throne. Elizabeth, of Protestant persuasion, once again broke away from the Catholic Church—restoring the Church of England to its former place of authority. Queen Elizabeth I, being more tolerant than her predecessor, offered some accommodation to England's Catholics.[4]

But for reform-minded Christians, the reign of Queen Elizabeth I left much to be desired. She reinstated the "Act of Supremacy," the law making her head of the Church of England. The Reformation had called into question the idea of a single person, with all power, ruling over the church. Additionally, it became mandatory in 1558 for everyone to attend church once a week or else pay a fine.[5] It was this environment that stirred the growth of the Puritan movement in England.

Puritans and Separatists

Puritans were people who wanted to purify the structure and practices of the Church of England. They were not seeking to overthrow the church, but to purify it from within.

Yet frustrations among the Puritans gave rise to a more bold approach to change—the Separatist movement. Separatists believed that if the Church of England could not be changed, they would separate from it to gather in private congregations, an illegal practice at that time. The movement grew significantly when Separatist leader Robert Browne published a document in 1582 titled, *"A Treatise of Reformation without Tarrying for Any."* In it, he made the case that the church should reform itself even if the governing authorities forbade it. His ideas became popular, being adopted by the Separatist congregation that the Pilgrims would come from.

King James and Two Billion Bibles

The death of Elizabeth I in 1603 leads us to King James I. He was King during the time the Pilgrims decided to leave England for Holland, and also when they later sailed to the New World on the Mayflower.

When King James took the throne, hopes were high that he might yield to the Puritans' request for greater reform of the church. The Puritans put together the Millenary Petition, a list of their desired reforms for James to consider. The King agreed to hear and debate the Puritans at the Hampton Court Conference of 1604. He was known to enjoy discussion and debate on theological topics, something the Puritans hoped would give their petition a chance.

The results of the conference were, in some ways, disappointing for the Puritans. James conceded to a few small reforms that were not at the heart of their petition. In other ways, the Hampton Court Conference produced astonishing results.

During the Puritans' discussion with the King, they voiced the need for a better English translation of the Bible. James, for reasons that included strengthening his rule, agreed. He considered the popular Geneva Bible to be "the worst of all"[6] translations, due to its inclusion of margin notes supporting less hierarchical church government. He eagerly commissioned

Figure 1: *King James I of England meets with Puritan leaders, and agrees on the need for a new translation of the Bible into English.*

the best minds from the academic and church worlds to produce a translation true to the original manuscripts. The King James Authorized Version was released in 1611. Still used today in an updated form, the King James Version of the Bible is the most printed book in history.[7] It is estimated that more than two billion copies have been made.[8]

More good would ultimately come from the conference, but through a process of trial and suffering.

Conform, or Else!

James discerned during discussions with the Puritans that they favored a change to the Church of England's form of government. It was true. Behind their politeness and respect, many Puritans did not like having a king rule the church through his regional bishops. King James was firm and direct in his response—he believed he should retain complete authority over the church. He knew that removing the control exercised through the bishops would diminish his authority, saying, "I know what would become of my supremacy. No Bishop, No King."[9]

That day at the conference did not end well for the Puritans. The King, being somewhat stirred, rose from his chair and brought the discussion to an end. His parting words were clear for those wanting greater religious liberty, "I shall make them conform themselves, or I will harry them out of this land, or else do worse."[10]

Purpose in the Midst of Persecution

The words of King James proved true.

As a result of his ongoing opposition to change, there would be a wave of people "harried out of the land." Among them, a small congregation on board the Mayflower. They would later demonstrate the power of their ideas in the wilderness of Massachusetts. The world was about to discover government with "no bishop, no king" and no state control of the church.

Against all odds, the faith and persistence of a small group of people was about to change the course of history.

Chapter Summary and Application

- "The king's heart is like channels of water in the hand of the LORD; He turns it wherever He wishes," says Proverbs 21:1.
- What does the Scripture above mean? Do our efforts and actions matter when faced with unjust and unrighteous rulers?
- Are you looking for the good that is being forged–against all odds–in the midst of today's trials and frustrations?

NOTES:

1. Parliament of England, *"Act of Supremacy,"* 1534.
2. Eugene Stock, *The Story of the Bible* (New York: E. P. Dutton and Company, 1906), 107.
3. This 1554 Act of Parliament provided authority for repressing heresies and punishing heretics.
4. The *Elizabethan Religious Settlement* sought to bring stability to England's religious turmoil.
5. Parliament of England, "*Act of Uniformity,"* 1558.
6. William Barlow, *The Summe and Substance of the Conference* (Clerkenwell: Bye and Law, 1804), 35.
7. *"April 22, 2011 ~ King James Bible 400th Anniversary."* PBS. Public Broadcasting Service, May 10, 2013. https://www.pbs.org/wnet/religionandethics/2011/08/05/april-22-2011-king-james-bible-400th-anniversary/8666/.
8. Jon Sweeney, *Verily, Verily: the KJV: 400 Years of Influence and Beauty,* (Grand Rapids: Zondervan, 2011).
9. Barlow, *The Summe and Substance of the Conference,* 62.
10. Ibid, 63.

Figure 1. *Sailing of the Mayflower,* A. Forestier, Public Domain.

Figure 2. *King James and the Puritans,* Public Domain.

8

The Mayflower and the Enola Gay

December 7, 1941, a date which will live in infamy," crackled the voice of President Franklin D. Roosevelt over radios all across America, as he explained how "the United States of America was suddenly and deliberately attacked by naval and air forces of the Empire of Japan."[1] Roosevelt's speech to a joint session of Congress was followed immediately by a declaration of war against Japan in response to the attack on Pearl Harbor.

The United States was now officially engaged in World War II.

War—the awful last resort for civil government in restraining evil actions—would end through force what could not be ended through diplomacy. Putting debates about the necessity and morality of how it was done aside, there is no question that it was the extreme use of force which finally brought World War II to an end.

In the early hours of August 6, 1945, the Enola Gay, a B-29 Superfortress bomber lifted off the North Field runway of Tinian Island in the Pacific. Loaded in the aircraft's bomb-bay was the first atomic weapon ever deployed in warfare.

1500 miles away, in Hiroshima, Japan, the stirrings of the early morning began as they never would again for more than 70,000 people. As they tossed and turned, got up to check their children, then prepared the day's first—and last—meal, something was coming across the ocean sky toward them.

What, exactly, was coming?

An airplane and a bomb? Yes, but in the most fundamental and grievous sense, it was government—not for the people of Hiroshima (and later Nagasaki) specifically, but government in the form of brute force for a totalitarian regime that would not cease hostilities by any other means. Less than a month later, on September 2, 1945, Japan formally surrendered on the deck of the USS Missouri in Tokyo Bay.

A Stunning Contrast

325 years earlier, something infinitely more gentle, something destined to promote preservation and peace was making its way across the ocean. It too was a form of government—not a bomb in the literal sense, but an idea with immensely powerful consequences. On September 6, 1620, the Mayflower, a small merchant ship, left the docks of Plymouth England. Loaded within the hearts and minds of a small group of passengers was the understanding of a new model of government soon to be deployed on the shores of their new home. It would help bring an end to the war on liberty that had been waged by kings and tyrants throughout most of history.

Who were these people, making their way across the Atlantic Ocean in the fall of 1620?

The unique passengers onboard the Mayflower, remembered today as the "Pilgrims," came from a Separatist church that formed around 1606, near the small village of Scrooby in north Nottinghamshire, England. They met covertly in the manor-house of William Brewster, an elder of the congregation who was also Scrooby's bailiff and postmaster.

Former Church of England minister John Robinson joined

Figure 1: *The "Scrooby Manor" where the Pilgrims met while in England.*

them, soon becoming their pastor, a position he would hold for many years. Robinson, describing his bold move to separate from the Church of England, wrote that he was motivated by the truth in his heart that was "as a burning fire shut up in my bones."[2]

Character, conviction, and courage. The Scrooby congregation's leadership were strong in these qualities. This was a wonderful work of divine providence, as the congregation would desperately need leaders with these qualities in order to fulfill their mission.

This congregation, and others across England, had been tested and tried by fire. Much of it came as the result of the appointment of a new Archbishop of Canterbury, Richard Bancroft, in 1604. Bancroft had long detested the Puritan and Separatist movements. The Earl of Clarendon said after Bancroft's death in 1610: "If Bancroft had lived, he would quickly have extinguished all that fire in England which had been kindled at Geneva,"[3] referring to the reverence Puritans and Separatists held for the Reformer John Calvin.

William Bradford

One remarkable member of the Scrooby fellowship was a boy named William Bradford. Orphaned by the loss of his father at age one, and his mother at age seven, he had been sent to live with his uncles.

The young Bradford became acquainted with William Brewster and other religious nonconformists and decided to join them. His uncles responded with wrath and his neighbors with scoffing. Bradford's response to them revealed much about the character and determination of this young man who would go on to become governor of Plymouth on the other side of the Atlantic:

> To keep a good conscience and walk in such a way as God has prescribed in his Word, is a thing which I must prefer before you all and above life itself. Wherefore since it is for a good cause that I am likely to suffer the disasters which you lay before me, you have no cause to be either angry with me, or sorry for me. Yea, I am not only willing to part with everything that is dear to me in this world for this Cause, but I am thankful that God hath given me heart so to do, and will accept me so to suffer for him.[4]

Along with solid character and leadership ability, Bradford's place among the Pilgrims added another dimension. He would become prolific in journaling the history of the Pilgrims while on both sides of the Atlantic. His best-known work, "Of Plymouth Plantation," is a gift to America of immense value. It describes in detail not just the places and events, but the motivations and beliefs that brought the Pilgrims to America. Historian Moses Coit Tyler goes so far as calling Bradford "The father of American history."[5]

The Journey Begins

Although willing to suffer, life in England became difficult for this congregation. Due to the heavy-handed government they were under, they could not live "a quiet and peaceable life in all godliness" (1 Timothy 2:2) but rather were "hunted and persecuted on every side."[6] Far from being in vain, their suffering became the very impetus that brought them and many others into liberty. In his 1813 account of this period, Benjamin Brook describes how the exodus of religious nonconformists began:

> Archbishop Bancroft incessantly harassed and plagued the Puritans to bring them to an exact conformity. On account of his rigorous proceedings, great numbers resolved to transport themselves to Virginia, and settle in that uncivilized country, where they could enjoy the blessing of religious liberty.[7]

Thus, in 1607, the "pilgrimage" of the Scrooby congregation began. For them, the first leg of the journey was not to Virginia, but Holland. Bradford recalls, "seeing...that there was no hope of their continuance there, by a joint consent they resolved to go to the Low-Countries, where they heard was freedom of religion for all men."[8]

This departure from England was not legally permitted. It required a secretive plan and the cooperation of ships and their captains, who more than once betrayed them in this process. On one occasion, after having boarded a ship with their possessions, they were ransacked, stripped of their money and property, and handed over to the authorities to be imprisoned. Along with many other distresses, William Bradford recorded that, "In the end, notwithstanding the storms of opposition, they all got over, some from one place, some from another, and met together again with no small rejoicing."[9] Finally settling in the university city of Leiden, this became their home for almost 12 years.

The Beloved John Robinson

Under the skillful care of Pastor John Robinson and Elder William Brewster, the church enjoyed sweet fellowship in Leiden, freely walking in the ways of God. In William Bradford's recollection of this time, he said of Pastor

Robinson, "It was hard to judge whether he delighted more in having such a people, or they in having such a pastor."[10] The community grew and flourished as others joined them from all over England.

Other aspects of life in Holland were not as favorable. Working conditions often took a physical toll on parents and their children, as families sought to make a living. Of more concern was the immorality of the Dutch youth. Many temptations surrounded the Pilgrims' children, leading some into destructive paths. Seeing that their "posterity would be in danger to degenerate and be corrupted"[11] prompted serious consideration of relocating elsewhere. After a season of careful prayer, research and discussion, it was decided—they would cross the Atlantic and settle in Virginia.[12]

Global Missionary Vision

The Pilgrims' vision of a new life in North America went beyond matters of employment and family. It was as if they were looking over the horizon, seeing something that stretched far into the future. William Bradford recounts their motivation while preparing to leave Holland:

> Last and not least, they cherished a great hope and inward zeal of laying good foundations, or at least of making some way towards it, for the propagation and advance of the gospel of the kingdom of Christ in the remote parts of the world, even though they should be but stepping stones to others in the performance of so great a work.[13]

This clarity of missionary vision is remarkable. They saw the remote parts of the earth as the final destination for the gospel, having no thought of Christianity becoming stagnant or self-absorbed in America. They knew the fulfillment of this vision would require multiple generations. They would do their part so that others, including you and I, could finish the task.

This clear sense of calling to America is something I can relate to, having come to America myself in response to the call of God. I remember all kinds of emotions and anxieties that had to be processed as I decided to leave my home country. I can only imagine how the Pilgrims felt—committing to take their families on an ocean voyage to a new life in the wilderness of another continent. Their story is inspiring. They suffered all the opposition, trials, setbacks, and weaknesses that are common to each of us. Yet in obedience to the call of God, their lives made a major contribution to this nation, and to the world.

I want to encourage you—as you sense God's calling on your life, "set your face like flint," and stay the course like the Pilgrims did. Through their influence and example, they truly are "stepping stones" for us as we go on to finish the task of presenting "the gospel of the kingdom of Christ in the remote parts of the earth."

A Platform for Reaching All Nations

We have seen that the Pilgrims explicitly aimed at "laying good foundations" for the fulfillment of global missionary purposes.

Usually, when we think of early missionary movements coming out of England, we rightly focus on William Carey. He was the English shoemaker turned missionary leader who stirred the church to engage in foreign missionary work through his provocative 1792 essay, "*An Enquiry into the Obligations of Christians to Use Means for the Conversion of the Heathens.*" He then led by example through his life's work as a missionary in India, earning him the title, "The Father of Modern Missions." While the Pilgrims did not start a missionary movement the same way Carey did, their vision helped lay the foundation for the most prolific missionary sending nation in history.

No Turning Back

Despite the dangers and difficulties of a move to North America, the majority of the Leiden congregation committed to the endeavor. Their answer to objections was that "all great and honourable actions are accompanied with great difficulties," and must be "overcome by answerable courage."[14]

Not the least of their challenges was the question of how to finance their move to another continent. After negotiations, funding for the voyage would come from the Pilgrims themselves and a group of investors, the London Merchant Adventurers. The investors expected to be repaid through shipments of timber, furs, and other commodities from the New World.

Not all the congregation were able to leave Holland on the first crossing. Though desiring to depart when they could, the majority remained in Leiden. Pastor Robinson would stay with them, it was decided, while Elder William Brewster went on the first journey.

When the heart-wrenching time of separation was upon them, Pastor John Robinson addressed those departing. Blessed with the ability to skillfully instruct and exhort, in his farewell address, Robinson revealed an insight with a prophetic air about it—a sense that something significant lay ahead of them.

Seeing Over the Horizon

In his address, Robinson pointed out that after the great change of the Reformation period, many churches had "come to a [standstill] in religion." The Lutherans, he said, "could not be drawn to go beyond what Luther saw," and "the Calvinists…they stick where he left them…For though they were precious shining lights in their times; yet God had not revealed his whole will to them."[15] It was Pastor Robinson's firm conviction that "the Lord had more truth and light yet to break forth out of his holy Word."[16]

He was right. It would not be many years before William Bradford—who became governor of the Plymouth settlement—would note concerning the influence of the Mayflower Compact and the model of government it demonstrated: "As one small candle may light a thousand, so

Figure 2: *The "Embarkation of the Pilgrims." A Painting displayed in the Rotunda of the Capitol Building in Washington, D.C.*

the light here kindled hath shone unto many, yea in some sort to our whole nation."[17] We will examine the fullness of this influence in the next chapter.

An Emotional Departure

Two ships were chosen for the Atlantic crossing. One, the Mayflower, was being prepared in Southampton, England. The other ship, the Speedwell, would bring the Pilgrims from the Dutch port of Delfshaven to Southampton, joining the Mayflower there for the departure to America. Describing the scene at Delfshaven at the moment the Pilgrims departed, William Bradford remembers:

> What sighs, and sobs, and prayers, did sound amongst them; what tears did gush from every eye…But the tide which stays for no man, calling them away...their reverand pastor falling down on his knees, and they all with him, with watery cheeks commended them with most fervent prayers to the Lord, and his blessing.[18]

The Mayflower and Speedwell set sail for the New World

on August 5, 1620. When the Speedwell began leaking, both ships stopped at Dartmouth for the repair. An attempt was made to resume the voyage on August 21. Around 300 miles out to sea, the Speedwell's leak once again forced both ships back to England, this time to Plymouth, a port city in England that ended up becoming the namesake for their settlement across the Atlantic. After the second leak, there would be no further attempt to take the Speedwell—the Mayflower would sail alone.

On September 6, 1620, the sails of the Mayflower caught a "prosperous wind,"[19] and the Pilgrims, though reduced in number, were on their way.

The Pilgrims were not the only ones on board the ship. There were the ship's crew as well as the traders and merchants who had come along to do business and earn profits. Seasickness and ferocious weather plagued the journey, as did a particular member of the ship's crew. This young sailor cursed the Pilgrims daily in the midst of their sickness, and as Bradford recalls, "did not hesitate to tell them that he hoped to help throw half of them overboard before they came to their journey's end."[20] Yet it was this sailor who was the first to die—struck by a grievous disease. His fellow crew members saw this with astonishment as being "the just hand of God upon him."[21]

Difficulties Overcome

At one point of the journey a major beam in the ship broke during a fierce storm. The Pilgrims were able to repair it using a giant screw jack they had fortunately brought along with them, most likely to help in building their homes in the New World.

The Mayflower itself was not the most suitable ship for a transatlantic voyage. The ship had a thirty foot high "aft-castle," consisting of the poop deck (from the French "la poupe," the stern of a ship), the captain's cabin, and the steerage room. This high structure made sailing against the

***Figure 2**: The "Mayflower II," a replica of the original Mayflower that carried the Pilgrims across the Atlantic.*

prevailing headwinds difficult, almost doubling the time at sea for the 102 passengers—all crammed into the gun deck, a space 24 feet wide, 58 feet long and just five and half feet high.

Though intending to make landfall at the Hudson River, near modern-day New York City, the storms had blown them about 200 miles to the north. Nevertheless, great joy filled their hearts at the first sight of land, which proved to be Cape Cod. When an attempt to sail southward was thwarted by treacherous waters, they returned northward, taking shelter within the Cape. This unexpected change of destination, however, would be a catalyst in bringing about a turning point in history.

Finally safe from the perils of their journey, "they fell upon their knees and blessed the God of heaven…"[22]

Though the ocean was now behind them—troubled waters lay ahead.

Chapter Summary and Application

- Do seemingly "small and insignificant" people have a place in changing the course of history?
- How many difficulties and trials are you willing to persevere through as you hold fast to your convictions?
- The Pilgrims knew they would be as "stepping stones" to others in reaching the whole world with the Gospel of Jesus Christ. How are you called to walk on those stepping stones?

NOTES:

1. Roosevelt, Franklin D. *Speech by Franklin D. Roosevelt, New York Transcript.* 1941. PDF. https://www.loc.gov/item/afccal000483/.
2. John Robinson, *The Works of John Robinson: Pastor of the Pilgrim Fathers, Vol. II.* (London, John Snow, 1851), 52.
3. George Perry, *A History of the Church of England: From the Accession of Henry VIII, to the Silencing of Convocation in the Eighteenth Century* (New York: Harper and Brothers, 1879), 371.
4. William Bradford, *Bradford's History of Plymouth Plantation, 1606-1646* (New York: Charles Scribner's Sons, 1920), 6.

5. Moses Coit Tyler, *A History of American Literature, Vol. I, 1606-1676* (New York: G.P. Putnam's Sons, 1879), 116.
6. Bradford, *Bradford's History of Plymouth Plantation,* 8.
7. Benjamin Brook, *The Lives of the Puritans: Containing a Biographical Account of Those Divines who Distinguished Themselves in the Cause of Religious Liberty from the Reformation Under Queen Elizabeth, to the Act of Uniformity in 1662, Vol. 1* (London, James Black, 1813), 64-65.
8. William Bradford, updated by Harold Paget, *Bradford's History of the Plymouth Settlement, 1608-1650* (New York: E. P. Dutton and Company, 1920), 8.
9. Ibid, 13.
10. Ibid, 16.
11. Ibid, 21.
12. Not Virginia as we know the state's borders today. "Virginia" was the name of England's first claim to a vast territory in the New World, out of which the original colonies, then states, eventually formed.
13. Bradford, *Bradford's History of the Plymouth Settlement, 1608-1650,* 21.
14. Ibid, 22.
15. John Robinson, *"Hypocrisy Unmasked,"* in The Harvard Theological Review, Vol. XIII (Cambridge: Harvard University Press, 1920), 236.
16. Ibid.
17. Bradford, *Bradford's History of the Plymouth Settlement, 1608-1650,* 226.
18. Ibid, 50.
19. Ibid, 62.
20. Ibid.
21. Ibid.
22. Ibid, 64.

Figure 1. *Scrooby Manor,* Public Domain.
Figure 2. *Embarkation of the Pilgrims,* Robert Walter Weir, Public Domain.
Figure 3. *Mayflower II,* Jim Curran, licensed for commercial use.

9

America's Covenant

The Mayflower rocked to and fro in the passing swells, anchored in the relative safety of what today is Provincetown Harbor, Cape Cod. Sixty-six days at sea had taken its toll. Sails and ropes were frayed, as were the nerves of the passengers and crew.

Mutiny Brews Among a Motley Crew

As mentioned previously, not everyone on the Mayflower was seeking religious freedom in the New World. Those from the Leiden church made up less than half of the 102 passengers. Others onboard included the ship's crew, and those recruited to work for the London Merchant Adventurers. Being thrown together to face a winter in the wilderness, "discontented and mutinous speeches"[1] were heard among them.

Adding to the tension was their change of destination. The Pilgrims had a "land patent"[2] from England, authorizing them to settle under the government of Virginia. Storms during their voyage had forced them northward into New England territory. Some were now saying "when they came ashore they would use their own liberty, for none had power to command them, the patent they had being for Virginia and not for New England, which belonged to another government, with which the Virginia Company had nothing to do."[3]

E Pluribus Unum (Out of Many, One)

Bringing order and unity to this diverse and distressed group became priority number one. But how, if at all, could this motley group be governed? The wisdom and foresight of the Pilgrim's pastor, John Robinson, would greatly help them during this challenging time. In his farewell letter, he exhorted the Pilgrims on the subject of civil government, stating in part:

> "Lastly, whereas you are become a body politic, using amongst yourselves civil government...let your wisdom and godliness appear, not only in choosing such persons as do entirely love and will promote the common good, but also in yielding unto them all due honor and obedience in their lawful administrations."[4]

The fruit of Robinson's instruction and admonition was remarkable. In an environment of physical exhaustion, simmering discontent, and a hostile winter before them, the question of government was settled. Before their feet touched the shores of the New World, they made a covenant, which defined their vision and purpose, and also established a framework for civil government. We refer to this covenant today as the Mayflower Compact, made November 11th, 1620. Bradford records it as "the first foundation of their government."[5]

Liberty Has a Stake in the Ground

The full text of the Mayflower Compact reads:

> IN THE NAME OF GOD, AMEN. We, whose names are underwritten, the Loyal Subjects of our dread Sovereign Lord King James, by the Grace of God, of Great Britain,

Figure 1: *The historic Mayflower Compact is signed before any passengers set foot on the shores of the New World.*

France, and Ireland, King, Defender of the Faith, &c. Having undertaken for the Glory of God, and **Advancement of the Christian Faith**, and the Honour of our King and Country, a Voyage to plant the first Colony in the northern Parts of Virginia; Do by these Presents, solemnly and mutually, in the Presence of God and one another, covenant and combine ourselves together into a civil Body Politick, for our better Ordering and Preservation, and **Furtherance of the Ends aforesaid**: And by Virtue hereof do enact, constitute, and frame, such just and equal Laws, Ordinances, Acts, Constitutions, and Officers, from time to time, as shall be thought most meet and convenient for the general Good of the Colony; unto which we promise all due Submission and Obedience. IN WITNESS whereof we have hereunto subscribed our names at Cape-Cod the eleventh of November, in the Reign of our Sovereign Lord King James, of England, France, and Ireland, the eighteenth, and of Scotland the fifty-fourth, Anno Domini; 1620.[6]

By the addition of signatures to the text shown above, something remarkable happened. A diverse group of people gave their consent to the form of government by which they would be ruled. The people, without the coercion of a king or queen, were ruling themselves. Their civil government would be no more and no less than was needed to provide their "ordering and preservation," and would set them at liberty to pursue "the furtherance of the ends" for which they had come to the New World.

Don't Ever Forget

For modeling such important elements of civil government, the Mayflower Compact has a prominent place among America's historical documents. At a ceremony laying the cornerstone for the Pilgrim Memorial Monument at Provincetown, President Theodore Roosevelt said, "The coming hither of the Pilgrim three centuries ago shaped the destinies of this continent, and therefore affected the destiny of the whole world."[7] He went on to say, "The Puritans' task was to…lay deep the immovable foundations of our whole American system of civil, political and religious liberty achieved through the orderly process of law."[8]

One of History's Big Stories Unfolds

The Pilgrims and their compact turned ideas about government upside down, or more properly, right-side up. For millennia past, government had been largely a power game. This problem echoes back to a tragic moment in history—when Israel asked God for a man to rule over them as king.

Israel was chosen to show the world God's intended way to do things, including concepts of government. Yet when Israel left Egypt, they had a slave mentality from four centuries under the Pharaohs. They needed to be taught, from the ground up, how to become a nation that could govern itself—a task that Moses was instrumental in performing under the guidance of God, and with input from his father-in-law.

Giving the people a basic framework for civil government, Moses directed them to have local representatives from each tribe, saying "Choose wise and discerning and experienced men from your tribes, and I will appoint them as your heads" (Deuteronomy 1:13). Moses taught all the people the statutes and the laws by which they were to live.[9] He then gave instructions to the leaders:

> Hear *the cases* between your fellow countrymen, and judge righteously between a man and his fellow countryman, or the alien who is with him. You shall not show partiality in judgment; you shall hear the small and the great alike. You shall not fear man, for the judgment is God's. The case that is too hard for you, you shall bring to me, and I will hear it. (Deuteronomy 1:16-17)

In the system being revealed to Israel, we see the idea of civil government being administrated at the local level as much as possible, by leaders the people had chosen from among themselves. The people's highest level of government—we learn in 1 Samuel 8—was not to be a great layer of bureaucracy, but rather their relationship with God as their king.

Jesus is King

To understand what is meant by God ruling as king, we can look to the life of Jesus, the King of Kings. Jesus did not come to be served, but to serve. He did not sacrifice his people for his own ends, but laid down his life to save theirs. If Israel would let God be king, especially over their hearts, then limited civil government and much liberty would be their twin blessings.

But as time passed, Israel did a foolish thing. They saw that the surrounding nations had a man for their king—and they wanted one too. "Give us a king!" they demanded of Samuel the prophet, who warned it was a bad idea to centralize power into one man's hands. They refused to listen, saying "There shall be a king over us, that we also may be like all the nations" (1 Samuel 8:19). God told Samuel, "They have rejected Me from being king over them" (1 Samuel 8:7). God let them have their king and all the consequences that came with it.

The Lost Model Returns

Thus the model of government Israel was supposed to share with the world vanished around 1000 BC. It would be 2600 years until it resurfaced in a substantive way, beginning with the Mayflower Compact in AD 1620, in the wilderness of New England. "It was an agreement or covenant or cooperative act from which was to spring not only a stable government for the little colony but a great series of constitutions for free states,"[10] noted Dr. Charles Eliot, the former President of Harvard University, speaking at the dedication of the Pilgrim Monument in 1910.

The preceding centuries had produced the understanding the Pilgrims needed for this moment. Ancient Israel had let their affections wander—losing sight of the liberty God intended for mankind. The Pilgrims set their affections on God, and would show the world that liberty in civil government is possible when your heart is already ruled by a higher authority.

Key Ideas in the Mayflower Compact

Why is the Mayflower Compact recognized as such an important historical document?

First, it defined the concept of self-rule, whereby the people constructed their own form of government, then consented to be governed by it. The people would participate in the lawmaking process and in the choosing of government officers. Although without a "patent" for New England, they believed a government of their own making "would be as effective as any patent and in some respects more so."[11] They successfully made a departure from the model of a monarchy, or other centralized form of government. Dr. Eliot observed that the Mayflower Pilgrims "founded and maintained a state without a king or a noble, and a church without a bishop or a priest."[12]

Second, the Mayflower Compact recognized that civil government was not the embodiment of life's highest purpose. The Pilgrims did not want to serve government almighty—they wanted to serve God Almighty. The Compact made it clear that government was to serve them. It was to facilitate their ordering and preservation, and the ability to live "for the glory of God, and advancement of the Christian faith." For most of history, rulers had believed their subjects existed to serve them and the state.

Third, the Mayflower Compact made a healthy distinction between the administration of civil government and church government. The Pilgrims had experienced in England the problems of a king as head of both church and state. While acknowledging God's purpose for government, the Mayflower Compact did not try to define the Pilgrims' church covenant, which they formed separately.

A Divine Equation

In the field of science, it is noted that the qualities of elegance and simplicity are often present in the correct explanation for a complex reality, as exemplified in the equation $E=mc^2$. It struck me as I looked at the Mayflower Compact, that a similar elegance and simplicity was present. Taking three powerful elements from the Mayflower Compact (explained in detail below), an "equation" describing the source of America's divine favor could be written as:

> America's Divine Favor = Living for the Glory of God + Fulfilling the Great Commission × Responsibility for Civil Government.

It is this convergence that forms the heart of the *20/20 Vision for America* message. If a handful of people helped change the world by forming a covenant around the three ideas in our "equation," imagine what will happen as believers in America remember those ideas, and re-covenant to fulfill them again today.

In the following chapters, each of the three points below is expanded into an action plan. Briefly, here is a summary:

1. **Living for the Glory of God**

   "Having undertaken for the Glory of God..." The Scripture says, "Whether, then, you eat or drink or whatever you do, do all to the glory of God" (1 Corinthians 10:31). To live for the glory of God is a foundational precept. Doing "all" for the glory of God touches everything. It instructs the way we think, vote, do business, speak, raise our children, and so on. It forms a template for personal and corporate revival, as we ask ourselves, "Is there anything in my life that does not glorify you, God?" Living for the glory of God has direct implications for America's national life: "Righteousness exalts a nation, but sin is a disgrace to any people" (Proverbs 14:34).

2. **Advancing the Christian Faith (The Great Commission)**

   "Advancement of the Christian faith..." In addition to living for God's glory in an overall sense, we have been given a very specific assignment by Jesus. He said, "Go therefore and make disciples of all the nations, baptizing them in the name of the Father and the Son and the Holy Spirit, teaching them to observe all that I commanded you; and lo, I am with you always, even to the end of the age" (Matthew 24:14). In God's economy, the blessing we receive as a nation is not given only for us, but for us to bless every other nation on earth with the message of his gospel and discipleship. God spoke to Abraham, "I will bless you…And in you all the families of the earth will be blessed" (Genesis 12:2-3). God has blessed America so that we can be a blessing.

3. Taking Responsibility for Civil Government

"[We] covenant and combine ourselves together into a civil Body Politick, for our better Ordering and Preservation, and Furtherance of the Ends aforesaid..." The apostle Paul explicitly connects civil government with freedom to fulfill God's purposes: "First of all, then, I urge that entreaties *and* prayers, petitions *and* thanksgivings, be made on behalf of all men, for kings and all who are in authority, so that we may lead a tranquil and quiet life in all godliness and dignity" (1 Timothy 2:1-2). Political liberty in America has produced astounding results in terms of "Advancing the Christian faith." America has been the most prolific missionary sending nation in history.

A Stone of Remembrance

The book of Judges records the account of the people of Israel crossing the Jordan river into "the promised land."[13] Like the Pilgrims, they were crossing a body of water to begin a new life. God parted the Jordan and the people crossed on dry land. They were to take 12 large stones from the river to remind them of what God had done. Joshua said that when their children ask, "What do these stones mean to you?" they were to recount the great things God had done that day.

The Pilgrim's story has something similar. "Plymouth Rock," in Plymouth, Massachusetts, is a symbolic memorial to the place the Mayflower passengers disembarked when they chose that location for their permanent settlement. Plymouth is the perfect place for a Stone of Remembrance. The harbor is shallow, never becoming the major port and economic center that Boston did. Plymouth has remained a quiet town where its history—its greatest asset—has not been overshadowed or swept away by centuries of economic development.

The story of the Pilgrims and the Mayflower Compact has been preserved for us to remember—for good reason.

Having "pulled back the bow" as discussed in chapter three, it's time to carefully take aim in the next three chapters, making application to what we have learned.

Chapter Summary and Application

- What role did personal character play in the success of the Mayflower Compact? Did everyone on the Mayflower have good character?
- What was the relationship between the goals of living "for the glory of God and advancement of the Christian faith," and their purpose for civil government?
- Why did "government by consent" have more power to rule than if one of them had tried to rule by force?

NOTES:

1. William Bradford, updated by Harold Paget, *Bradford's History of the Plymouth Settlement, 1608-1650* (New York: E. P. Dutton and Company, 1920), 75.
2. A "land patent" was a legal document issued by the English government, granting permission to settle on land in the New World under English controlled local government.
3. Bradford, *Bradford's History of the Plymouth Settlement*, 75.
4. Ibid, 55.
5. Ibid, 75.
6. F. Newton Thorpe, *The Federal and State Constitutions, Colonial Charters, and Other Organic Laws of the State, Territories, and Colonies Now or Hertofore Forming the United States of America* (Washington: Government Printing Office, 1909), 1841.
7. President Theodore Roosevelt, *"Address of President Roosevelt on the occasion of the laying of the cornerstone of the Pilgrim Monument"* (Speech at Provincetown, Massachusetts, August 20, 1907).
8. Ibid.
9. Exodus 18:20.
10. Dr. Charles Eliot, *"Principal Address at the Dedication for the Pilgrim Monument, August 5, 1910,"* in *The Pilgrims and their Monument,* Edmund J. Carpenter (New York: D. Appleton and Company, 1911), 183.

11. Bradford, *Bradford's History of the Plymouth Settlement,* 75.
12. Eliot, *The Pilgrims and their Monument,* 182.
13. Joshua 4.

Figure 1. *The Mayflower Compact,* Jean Leon Gerome Ferris, Public Domain.

SECTION TWO

America's Future

10

Main Application—Point One: Live for the Glory of God

From the Mayflower Compact:
"Having undertaken for the glory of God..."

From Scripture:
Tell of His glory among the nations, His wonderful deeds among all the peoples. For great is the LORD, and greatly to be praised. (1 Chronicles 16:24-25)

When Stephen and his family arrived at our ministry center in Texas, we all knew they were on a mission. Stephen's big smile and warm personality were a perfect match for what they were preparing to do—to make the love of God known to a people who don't believe he loves them.

After a few years of training, team building and logistical preparation, it was time for the big move. I remember how exciting it was as we prayed for this team, heading to a part of the world where few people are willing to go—a nation I cannot mention for security reasons.

Stephen and the team got a great work started in the capital city. The learning center they set up teaches skills to the local people, equipping them to have a better future. Just as we loved having Stephen in Texas, it wasn't long before he and his team were loved by their new community.

One morning some years ago, I received a phone call. The trembling voice on the other end was Stephen's father. He was giving us the shocking news he had gotten just moments before—Stephen had been murdered in a terrorist attack outside the training center.

A shockwave of grief hit us all. As we prayed for Stephen's family and the team, we remembered something Stephen had often said. When asked about the dangers he and his family faced living in a violent foreign land, his answer was a profound challenge: "We laid down our lives before going there."

In the years since his death, Stephen and his family have been greatly honored in the nation where he died. The work continues to flourish and so does his family. In the center of the nation's capital there is now a memorial to Stephen's life. It reads, "God is Love," forever proclaiming the message brought there by a young man who chose to live for the glory of God.

How Do We Give God Glory?

Most of us will probably not face what Stephen faced, but we are called to glorify God too. What does it mean then, for you and me to live for the glory of God?

To start with, we need to see that God is worthy of glory.

Moses asked God, "Show me Your glory!"

The Lord replied, "I Myself will make all My goodness pass before you" (Exodus 33:18). The Lord then hid Moses in the cleft of a rock, covering him with his hand as he passed by, allowing Moses to see only his back, but not his face.

Think about that. The glory of God shown to Moses was God's goodness—an attribute of his character. Even so, Moses' flesh and blood could only handle a partial exposure to the glory of God.

While our capacity is finite, we can know God—through his word, and by walking in relationship with him. In walking with God, Moses learned that God is "compassionate and gracious, slow to anger, and abounding in lovingkindness and truth; who keeps lovingkindness for thousands, who forgives iniquity, transgression and sin" (Exodus 34:5-7).

To glorify God then, is to know him—and to recognize, to enjoy, to put on display, to highly esteem, and to make known his glorious attributes.

The following points are important aspects of living for God's glory:

1. Clean Hands and a Pure Heart

> Who may ascend into the hill of the Lord? And who may stand in His holy place? He who has clean hands and a pure heart. (Psalm 24:3-4)

King David knew God as "The King of Glory" (Psalm 24:7). In his desire to honor and draw closer to God, he prayed, "Search me, O God, and know my heart...and see if there is any wicked way in me" (Psalm 139:23-24 KJV).

With honesty like David's, we too can ask, "God, is there anything in my life that does not glorify you?" He will be faithful to show us what needs attention, and in his kindness, patience, and mercy, he will lead us to repentance. David describes his experience of going through this process:

> When I kept silent about my sin, my body wasted away through my groaning all day long. For day and night Your hand was heavy upon me; my vitality was drained away as with the fever heat of summer. I acknowledged my sin to You, and my iniquity I did not hide; I said, "I will confess my transgressions to the LORD"; and You forgave the guilt of my sin. (Psalm 32:3-5)

It is a wonderful thing to experience forgiveness and a clean conscience.

No Skeletons in the Closet

I remember the peace I felt as the wheels of the Boeing 747 lifted off the tarmac at Auckland airport in 1995. I had some heavy bags in the cargo hold of the plane, but was thankful for the baggage that was not coming with me.

In 1994, I had completed a Discipleship Training School with Youth With A Mission, in Lindale, Texas. Having gone back to New Zealand for a short time after the training school, I was now in the process of moving to Texas permanently.

During this time, I felt God awaken my conscience to things I needed to deal with before my departure. The truth is, some of what God was pointing out I just wanted to forget—things that had not been glorifying to God, but quite the opposite. I ended up spending several hours just sitting before God, writing down what he showed me.

One issue concerned a man who had severely dishonored my father during the years he was suffering from Alzheimer's disease. As I had observed this man taking advantage of my father's situation, I developed a deep hatred for him. On one occasion, I took out vengeance by destroying a piece of his property he had left at our home, never telling him I had done it.

As I let God examine my heart, I knew I needed to make restitution for what I had done. Having now received some discipleship, I was able to see there were better ways I could have responded to the situation. What this man had done was still wrong, but I had chosen to do wrong in response. After praying about what to do, I took time to find the value of the item I had destroyed, then sent the man a letter along with a check to make things right.

In going through this process, I knew I was not earning my salvation or God's grace, but there was something wonderful about learning to be honest before God.

Many of the things on my list were appropriately settled between me and God. Others required meeting with or calling people to ask forgiveness, or to show honor and thankfulness that had been lacking. Some things were embarrassing to deal with, some very expensive. But the thrill of leaving New Zealand with a clean conscience was the most wonderful feeling.

From Glory to Glory

Of course, letting God examine and refine us is a lifelong process. But King David knew that God desires to do that with each of us, saying, "You desire truth in the innermost being," (Psalm 51:6). The result is that our lives will reflect the glory of God in an increasing way. As the Scripture says, "But we all, with unveiled face, beholding as in a mirror the glory of the Lord, are being transformed into the same image from glory to glory" (2 Corinthians 3:18).

2. Relationships and Sexual Morality

Walk in a manner worthy of the God who calls you into His own kingdom and glory. (1 Thessalonians 2:12)

While the very concept of sexual morality and purity is mocked today by many, the Bible has something truly wonderful to say on this subject—but we often miss it.

Sometimes, when Christians are asked why they believe something in this category is moral or immoral, the answer is simply, "Because it says so in the Bible." While this is good and right at one level, to those seeking understanding, it is hardly a complete answer. It gives the impression that Christians believe in an arbitrary set of prohibitions found in the Bible, while failing to explain that there are very good reasons for those prohibitions.

However, the definition of sexual morality and marriage in Scripture is anything but arbitrary. Among many other things, it protects from heartbreak, defines family, promotes commitment, and ensures that children have parents. At the same time, a much bigger dimension is revealed.

The Apostle Paul says something very insightful in his letter to the Ephesians. After speaking at some length about marriage, he makes a brief comment, "This mystery is great;

but I am speaking with reference to Christ and the church" (Ephesians 5:32). Paul seems to catch a glimpse here of the grandeur of our eternal relationship with Christ that is foreshadowed by the model of marriage—calling the mystery *great.* Coupled with numerous other verses making the same connection, this little comment from Paul, I believe, is of enormous importance today.

Why might it matter then, that gender has a definition, that marriage has a definition and that the boundaries of sexual relationships have definition? If God is wanting marriage to be a model that points to something utterly magnificent—his relationship with us throughout eternity—then no wonder there are powers at work to corrupt, distort, pervert, and destroy that model and everything associated with it!

It is common in Scripture for a complex concept to be introduced through a smaller, more easily understood model, which prepares the way for something greater. An example would be the sacrificial system in the Old Testament, where innocent animals such as unblemished lambs were sacrificed. This shedding of innocent blood was to cleanse the sin of the people. It was meant to be shocking—to illustrate the awful cost of atonement for sin.

But a sacrificial lamb was just the model, pointing to the coming of Jesus, the sinless "Lamb of God." Jesus, in the ultimate demonstration of God's love, allowed himself to be sacrificed—suffering in our place to uphold justice, while making a way for mercy.

Gender, Sexuality, and Marriage

Given that Scripture reveals the foreshadowing of something very special through God's creation of gender, sexuality, and the relationship of marriage—what then are we to see? For some, the answer to this question is clouded by the experience of heartbreak and human failure. Some see nothing but the source of their anger and bitter grief, or a set of arbitrary mandates and prohibitions. I would like to suggest, however, that we are meant to see and even experience something that touches the deepest longing of the human soul.

The need to be wanted, protected, cherished, and delighted in, is something we all have from the moment of conception. We were created to be loved and to love. This love is meant to last through riches or poverty, sickness or health, and the best or worst of times. All of us long for—or at one time longed for—the kind of love that does not break our hearts.

The wisdom of God urges caution and restraint before giving our heart away, "Watch over your heart with all diligence, for from it flow the springs of life" (Proverbs 4:23). Far from restricting what is good, God's instructions prohibit us from trashing the hearts of others, and them from trashing ours. The intended fulfillment of intimate relationship between male and female is therefore found within the bonds of commitment—specifically the covenant of marriage.

"Blessed are those who are invited to the marriage supper of the Lamb," the Scripture tells us (Revelation 19:9). God is calling us to the unfathomable wonder of an eternal relationship with him which he describes as a marriage, where we need have no fear of his unfaithfulness or of his love failing us.

Let's honor the instructions God has given us out of his amazing goodness and love.

> Flee immorality. Every *other* sin that a man commits is outside the body, but the immoral man sins against his own body. Or do you not know that your body is a temple of the Holy Spirit who is in you, whom you have from God, and that you are not your own? For you have been bought with a price: therefore glorify God in your body. (1 Corinthian 6:18-20)

3. Love All the Peoples of the Earth

My house will be called a house of prayer for all the peoples.
(Isaiah 56:7)

The Bible teaches us, "Do not be overcome by evil, but

overcome evil with good" (Romans 12:21). One of the evils America must continue to overcome is that of enmity and dishonor between different racial groups. This has brought deep wounds, great tragedy and suffering to this nation, especially to African Americans and Native Americans.

This evil can be overcome. There can be a healing of America's wounds.

To harbor a wrong attitude toward a certain ethnic group is to be in opposition to God. He blessed Abraham so that "all the families of the earth" would be blessed (Genesis 12:3). Jesus died "for the sins of the whole world" (1 John 2:2 KJV). God's desire is for people "from every nation and all tribes and peoples and tongues" to worship before him (Revelation 7:9).

Having worked in a missionary organization for a long time, I have had the blessing of being surrounded by people from all over the world. Many have become close friends. It has been natural in this environment to learn to celebrate and delight in the ethnicities of the world. However, I remember the beginnings of this process of getting closer to unknown and unfamiliar people groups.

Taiwan was the location of my very first mission trip, part of the Discipleship Training School I attended with YWAM. As I sat on the airplane crossing the Pacific Ocean, I recall thinking, "I have more apprehension in my heart than love for the people of Taiwan." But after six weeks of working with, eating with, and befriending people in Taiwan, that changed forever. On the plane returning to the USA my thoughts were, "I love the people of Taiwan! I am going to miss them!"

There is unfinished business in America regarding relationships among different races. I would like to suggest that more than just "reconciliation" needs to happen. Reconciliation is a wonderful word and concept, yet it can give the impression of doing "just enough," or the minimum required to make peace with someone. God's standard for relating to our fellow man is to love, with sincerity of heart.

Let's reach out to intentionally spend time with and befriend people of different races and nationalities. We can be part of healing the wounds of the past, and in the process discover the joy that God intended there to be among the "families of the earth."

4. Walk Closely with God

This is eternal life, that they may know You, the only true God, and Jesus Christ whom You have sent. (John 17:3)

I asked a friend what she thought it meant to glorify God. Her answer was delightful. She said it is to be who you are truly made to be, then gave the example of a sunset. She said, "A sunset gives glory to God…by setting!"

Who are we truly made to be? The verse above indicates, along with many others, that we were made to know God, and to walk in a close relationship with Him. The Bible tells us, "Draw near to God and He will draw near to you" (James 4:8).

Describing the nature of our relationship further, Jesus explained, "I am the vine, you are the branches; he who abides in Me and I in him, he bears much fruit, for apart from Me you can do nothing...My Father is glorified by this, that you bear much fruit, and so prove to be My disciples" (John 15:5-8).

As we walk closely with God, with a desire to be near him and to know him, we not only fulfill who we were made to be, but our lives become fruitful. As this happens, it brings glory to God.

5. Good Character and Integrity

We have regard for what is honorable, not only in the sight of the Lord, but also in the sight of men. (2 Corinthians 8:21)
Righteousness exalts a nation, but sin is a reproach to any people. (Proverbs 14:34)

The Pilgrims, who stated in the Mayflower Compact that they came to America "for the glory of God," gave us a great example of how they glorified God through their character and integrity while still living in Holland:

> Though many of them were poor, there were none so poor but that if they were known to be of that congregation, the Dutch (either bakers or others) would trust them to any reasonable extent when they lacked money to buy what they needed. They found by experience how careful they were to keep their word, and saw how diligent they were in their callings, that they would even compete for their custom, and employ them in preference to others.[1]

What do people think of you and me as they interact with us in the everyday areas of work and business? Does our reputation in matters of character and integrity bring glory to God?

"In all things show yourself to be an example of good deeds, with purity in doctrine, dignified, sound in speech which is beyond reproach, so that the opponent will be put to shame, having nothing bad to say about us" (Titus 2:7-8).

6. Seek God's Glory, Not Your Own

Not to us, O LORD, not to us, But to Your name give glory Because of Your lovingkindness, because of Your truth. (Psalm 115:1)

If in the early 17th century, a think tank in England had been assigned the task of choosing people to lay a foundation for liberty in the New World, it is unlikely the Pilgrims would have been picked. How is it then, that they and the Mayflower Compact are now famous?

The secret is found in understanding greatness from God's perspective.

The Tower of Babel

Genesis chapter eleven tells the famous story of the Tower of Babel. The people desired to build a city with a great tower, "whose top *will reach* into heaven." Stating their motivation, they said, "Let us make for ourselves a name, otherwise we will be scattered abroad over the face of the whole earth."

The story is quite comical in two ways. First, concerning the tower's height reaching into heaven, we read, "The Lord *came down* to see the city and the tower which the sons of men had built." God had to come down to see it—obviously it hadn't reached as high as they had imagined! Second, God's purpose was to have mankind "fill the earth."[7] They did not want to do that. Instead, they sought to do the exact opposite of what God instructed them to do, so he intervened.

He confused their language, the building project stopped, and he "scattered them abroad over the face of the whole earth," the very thing they sought to avoid. These people sought to make their own name great—to seek their own glory. That is why they found themselves opposed by God.

The Calling of Abraham

Standing in stark contrast to those who sought their own glory is the account of God calling Abraham to follow him. Interestingly, this is found in Genesis chapter twelve, immediately following the Tower of Babel story. God said to Abraham, "Go forth from your country, and from your relatives and from your father's house, to the land which I will show you; And I will make you a great nation, and I will bless you, and make your name great…"

God said he would make Abraham's name great! There could not be two more opposite paths to a "great name" than these two stories illustrate. One way is to live for your own glory and fame, the other is to live for God's glory and fame, letting your reputation rest in God's hands. In this fundamental lesson from history, we see the greatness pursued at the Tower of Babel being thwarted by God, while the greatness Abraham does not seek is freely given to him by God.

Abraham is, by any account, one of the great names in history. Judaism, Christianity, and Islam all share "Abrahamic" roots. In Christianity, Abraham is called our "father in the faith." Why didn't Abraham seek the greatness of his own name? A clue is found when his story is repeated in the New

Testament. We read, "The God of glory appeared to our father Abraham when he was in Mesopotamia, before he lived in Haran, and said to him, 'Leave your country…' "

Abraham had seen the glory of God. When he compared his knowledge of God with his knowledge of himself, he obviously made a smart choice; he chose to trust and obey God's word above his own ways. In so doing, he became the patriarch God used to reveal his glory to the whole world.

Let's ask ourselves, are we trying to build a name for ourselves, motivated by vanity and pride? Are we using our strength and the days we've been given to build things that God will ultimately have to oppose, like the Tower of Babel? Or are we choosing, like so many men and women before us, to make God and his wonderful attributes famous throughout the earth?

Scripture tells us, "The earth will be filled with the knowledge of the glory of the Lord, as the waters cover the sea" (Habakkuk 2:14). Let's cooperate with God to see this happen quickly.

7. Know and Promote the Word of God

And the Word became flesh, and dwelt among us, and we saw His glory, glory as of the only begotten from the Father, full of grace and truth. (John 1:14)

Should you ever need a good reason to read and take the authority of Scripture seriously, here is one: Jesus did. Here are a few of the numerous examples showing how the Son of God thought about and related to the Word of God:

- "It is written..." Jesus declared, as he quoted Scripture to refute the devil's temptations (Matthew 4:10).
- "You are mistaken, not understanding the Scriptures nor the power of God" responded Jesus, when a sect known as the Sadducees tried to prove Jesus wrong with a flawed argument (Matthew 22:29).

- "Today this Scripture has been fulfilled in your hearing," Jesus announced, affirming the truth of Isaiah 61:1 (Luke 4:21).
- "[Jesus] took the twelve aside and said to them, 'Behold, we are going up to Jerusalem, and all things which are written through the prophets about the Son of Man will be accomplished.' "

It is impossible to study the life of Jesus without seeing that he viewed Scripture as a reference point for truth. A student is not greater than his master. For us to know who God is, who we are, and what glorifies him, we need to know the Bible well.

Jesus brought glory to God during his time on earth. He said, "I glorified You on the earth, having accomplished the work which You have given Me to do" (John 17:4). The work Jesus did included his study of Scripture. We can glorify God by doing the same.

8. Pray

Devote yourselves to prayer, keeping alert in it with an attitude of thanksgiving. (Colossians 4:2)

There is clearly a spiritual dimension to the battle over America's future. The Bible tells us that Satan does not want people to see the glory of God, "The god of this world has blinded the minds of the unbelieving so that they might not see the light of the gospel of the glory of Christ, who is the image of God" (2 Corinthians 4:4).

However, we can pray. "The weapons of our warfare are not carnal, but mighty through God to the pulling down of strong holds…destroying speculations and every lofty thing raised up against the knowledge of God" (2 Corinthians 10:4).

As America takes living for the glory of God seriously, we can be expectant of powerful changes to the whole nation. The well-known Scripture in 2 Chronicles 7:14 is an amazing promise. God says, "If My people who are called by My name humble themselves and pray and seek My face and turn from their wicked ways, then I will hear from heaven, will forgive their sin and will heal their land." May it be that we see the "healing" of America in our generation.

Summary

What is God showing you from the points above? Be obedient to what he makes known to you. In doing so, your life will find a closer alignment with the purpose for which you were created.

There is perhaps no more magnificent statement about the relationship between our purpose and the glory of God than the following, taken from the Westminster Shorter Catechism, a document produced by the Church of Scotland in 1648:

> *What is the chief end of man? Man's chief end is to glorify God, and to enjoy him forever.*

Let's do exactly that.

NOTES:

1. William Bradford, updated by Harold Paget, *Bradford's History of the Plymouth Settlement, 1608-1650* (New York: E. P. Dutton and Company, 1920), 17.

11

Main Application—Point Two: Advance the Christian Faith

From the Mayflower Compact: "Advancement of the Christian faith."

From Scripture: "Go and make disciples of all nations." (Matthew 28:19)

God bless America.

This phrase is seen and heard everywhere in this nation. In various forms, it is used by Presidents in their speeches, in patriotic songs, and on everything from souvenirs to bumper stickers. Whether anyone thinks about it much or not, America has acknowledged the connection between God and blessing.

But what is the connection? America has invented many things, but the concept of God and blessing is not an American invention. It is something that has been evident from the very beginning, as we read in the first book of the Bible, "God created man in His own image, in the image of God He created him; male and female He created them. God blessed them; and God said to them, "Be fruitful and multiply…" (Genesis 1:27-

28).

The first thing God did after creating men and women in his image—before asking them to do anything—was to bless them! Right from the start we see this pattern: God blesses first; then out of his blessing, he calls us to action.

Blessing can include material wealth, but is infinitely more than that. In his Sermon on the Mount, Jesus described some surprising aspects of blessing—such as the blessing of being poor in spirit, yet possessing the kingdom of heaven. He described the blessing of a great reward in heaven that is ours when people insult and persecute us because of our love for him.

At the same time, God himself does speak of blessing "your basket and your kneading bowl," and of "making you abound in prosperity," and blessing "all the work of your hand" (Deuteronomy 28:5-12).

The Purpose of Blessing

So, if God has blessed America, how has he called us to action? There is a direct line revealed in the Bible between blessing and the revelation of God's love and redemption reaching others. It is expressed in numerous ways, such as Jesus saying "As I have loved you…love one another" (John 13:34), "Freely you have received, freely give" (Matthew 10:8 NKJV), and the Apostle Paul's exhortation that we "comfort those who are in any affliction with the comfort with which we ourselves are comforted by God" (2 Corinthians 1:4).

The scope of God's call to action goes beyond blessing those immediately around us. He calls us to also think in terms of all nations, every language, all peoples, etc. To see this more clearly, we will step back for a moment, and look at the big story into which we are called.

Abraham and the Big Picture of Blessing

Abraham, whose influence we have previously examined, was instrumental in revealing one of the grand narratives of history: God loves and desires to reconcile *all* the people of the earth to himself.

Abraham came from a completely pagan, idol-worshipping background in the region of Mesopotamia that is today Iraq. His life was a journey of learning to trust God and his words. Abraham is called our "Father in the faith" because he believed the promise God made to him, that although he was childless, he would have a son of his own as his heir:

> "...one who will come forth from your own body, he shall be your heir." And He took him outside and said, "Now look toward the heavens, and count the stars, if you are able to count them." And He said to him, "So shall your descendants be." Then he believed in the Lord; and He reckoned it to him as righteousness. (Genesis 15:4-6)

The birth of Abraham and Sarah's promised son came to pass, and he named him Isaac. Isaac became the father of Jacob, who was later called Israel. Thus Abraham became the great patriarch of the nation of Israel. Most importantly, it is from his descendants that Jesus the Messiah was born.

Look closely at how God first called Abraham (originally called Abram):

> Now the LORD said to Abram,
> "Go forth from your country,
> And from your relatives
> And from your father's house,
> To the land which I will show you;
> And I will make you a great nation,
> And I will bless you,
> And make your name great;
> And so you shall be a blessing;
> And I will bless those who bless you,
> And the one who curses you I will curse.
> And in you all the families of the earth will be
> blessed." (Genesis 12:1-3)

God said he would bless Abraham, and through Abraham, all the world would be blessed. Today, like the stars God showed Abraham, billions of people have chosen to trust God as Abraham did, including a majority of Americans. As Scripture says:

> Even so Abraham BELIEVED GOD, AND IT WAS RECKONED TO HIM AS RIGHTEOUSNESS. Therefore, be sure that it is those who are of faith who are sons of Abraham. The Scripture, foreseeing that God would justify the Gentiles by faith, preached the gospel beforehand to Abraham, *saying,* "ALL THE NATIONS WILL BE BLESSED IN YOU." So then those who are of faith are blessed with Abraham, the believer. (Galatians 3:6-9)

Jesus himself is the ultimate fulfillment of the blessing promised to Abraham. Galatians 3:29 says, "And if you are Christ's, then you are Abraham's offspring, heirs according to promise."

Jesus' Great Commission

Jesus, then, took the idea of blessing "All the nations of the earth" to another level. After his death and resurrection, Jesus gave final instructions to his disciples before ascending into heaven:

> All authority in heaven and on earth has been given to Me. Therefore go and make disciples of all nations, baptizing them in the name of the Father, and of the Son, and of the Holy Spirit, and teaching them to obey all that I have commanded you. And surely I am with you always, to the very end of the age. (Matthew 28:18-20)

This mandate from Jesus, the "Great Commission," is the task he has given us to complete before he returns. Making this abundantly clear, Jesus said, "This gospel of the kingdom shall be preached in the whole world as a testimony to all the nations, and then the end will come" (Matthew 24:14).

By including "Advancement of the Christian faith" in the Mayflower Compact, the Pilgrims aligned themselves with

God's central purpose for this time in history. Their vision, as already mentioned, was "of laying good foundations, or at least of making some way towards it, for the propagation and advance of the gospel of the kingdom of Christ in the remote parts of the world."

Fulfillment of the Vision

It is astounding to recognize that 400 years after the Pilgrims made their covenant with the goal of advancing the Christian faith, America is sending more missionaries than any other nation. Statistics for the year 2010 show that of the 400,000 missionaries sent by all nations combined, 127,000 were sent from America.[1] While it is not a competition (we are to champion missionaries out of every nation), Jesus said you will know a tree by its fruit. The "tree" of America has many examples of roots that are firmly grounded—like the Pilgrims' covenant—in the heart of God's purposes for the world.

I cannot present the challenge strongly enough on this point. A central reason for writing this book is to call America to continue, with greater intentionality than ever, to pursue the completion of the Great Commission.

The faith of those who have gone before us has produced a highly favorable environment in which to fulfill the task Jesus has given us. "Blessed is the nation whose God is the Lord," the Psalmist tells us (Psalm 33:12). America has been blessed with the liberty, opportunity, knowledge, and resources to do anything we put our minds to. The enormous list of American inventions, including airplanes, telephones, and computer chips, is a testament to that fact. While this leads some to attack America's wealth and influence in the world, the real problem is not with having these blessings—but with not knowing the purpose for which they were given.

What is Wrong with the American Dream?

Jesus explained how we are to think if we have been entrusted with great blessing: "From everyone who has been given much, much will be required" (Luke 12:48).

The concept of the American Dream embodies the idea we have been discussing. Many generations have seen the opportunity in America to rise from their current circumstances to something better. They have dreamed of and then seen their children have a better life than they had, after they seized their own opportunity to succeed in America. This is the natural and legitimate dream people have when they see a city on a hill—a place that has been blessed like America. Yet for some, the American Dream is seen as the endless pursuit of material wealth, with no clear purpose beyond personal pleasure and satisfaction.

For this reason, when I am speaking to a Christian audience, I like to ask the question: "What is wrong with the American Dream?" People get a little nervous for a moment, expecting the concept will be put down. But the answer I give them is, "It's not big enough!" If your dream is to have a house with a four-car garage, that is great. But God's dream will not fit in a four-car garage! The scope of our dreams needs to be more on the scale of God's plan and purpose for us.

God's Dream for All Nations

When God describes his dream—his unswerving purpose and the desire of his heart for the world—he uses the words "all" and "every."

- Go into *all* the world and preach the gospel to *every* creature (Mark 16:15 NKJV)
- Therefore go and make disciples of *all* nations…teaching them to obey *all* that I have commanded you. (Matthew 28:19-20)
- After these things I looked, and behold, a great multitude which no one could count, from *every* nation and *all* tribes and peoples and tongues, standing before the throne and before the Lamb (Revelation 7:9)

Nobody is left out of God's dream! It is a dream that

includes America, but reaches to the remotest parts of the earth. It can inspire someone with a four-car garage to join a four-camel caravan—delivering Bibles across the Gobi Desert of Mongolia. It reaches those living on your street at home and those on the mountainous, dusty trails of Central Asia.

Many people are thinking big in this age of globalism. But I challenge you to think big, and to think globally, by pursuing the heavenly dream Jesus has for the world. His dream is that "All the ends of the earth will remember and turn to the Lord, And all the families of the nations will worship before [the Lord]" (Psalm 22:27).

So how close are we to reaching all the world, and every creature? At the time of writing:

- The world population is approximately 7.7 billion.[2]
- Approximately 3.2 billion people are considered unreached by the message of the gospel of Jesus.[3]
- There are approximately 10,257 distinct people groups in the world.[4]
- 4433 distinct people groups are unreached by the message of the gospel of Jesus.[5]
- An estimated 1650 - 2100 vital languages have no Scripture translation yet.[6]

So, where do we begin in the great task of "advancing the Christian faith," as the Pilgrims put it?

Listen and Obey

Take time to pray, remembering that "Unless the LORD builds the house, they labor in vain who build it." (Psalm 127:1). Ask God, "How am I to take what you have blessed me with, and be a blessing to others? How am I to help fulfill the Great Commission?" Perhaps this is not your usual practice—asking God a question with the expectation of an answer. I want to encourage you that you will get an answer. You will probably even get multiple confirmations of God's answer. God says, "Call to Me and I will answer you, and I will tell you great and mighty things, which you do not know" (Jeremiah 33:3).

Making Disciples at Home and at School

Our task is to both preach the gospel—bringing people into relationship with God—and to make disciples of all nations. Jesus said we are to teach the nations "to observe all that I have commanded you" (Matthew 28:19). That teaching begins, of course, here in America as we raise and educate each generation.

For this reason, America must never lose the liberty that promotes—not just allows—private education. Education is first of all the domain of the family. The Bible teaches, "Train up a child in the way he should go..." (Proverbs 22:6). Education is also the domain of the church, as Jesus made obvious. While education goes far beyond church doctrines, education needs an objective basis for truth—something the biblical worldview has been hugely successful in providing.

Christianity has been a massive driver of literacy and education worldwide. Medieval monasteries promoted literacy and preserved literature. The Reformation popularized the idea of literacy as a necessity—to enable reading of the Bible. Multitudes of universities, over many centuries, have been established as an outgrowth of the church, including the likes of Harvard and Yale. Many tens of thousands of schools have resulted from Christian missionary activity throughout the world—expanding education to women and minorities in the process.[7]

The Bible is Essential to Education

America needs to remember this history. The Bible is not out of place in the classroom—the controlling hand of government is. Education in America began and prospered out of the domain of strong families and churches. Of course, a free people can together choose to direct tax money toward aspects of education. But we the people in America have largely lost control of education—by believing it to be primarily a function of government.

If America's foundational understanding of human rights, private property, government, law, justice, ethics, education, and family came from the Bible, how can America be educated in these vital foundations when teaching from the Bible is banned in most classrooms? It cannot.

While being salt and light in public schools is important, so is the expansion of quality private education where there is freedom to teach a biblical worldview. 20/20 Vision for America must include this goal if America is to be discipled as a nation and to be restored to health. A major reform of education is needed—but will only come about if there is an awakening among Christian families, educators, and influencers who pursue it.

There is room for great innovation here. Coupling technology with new paradigms is something America excels at. Once a successful new trend in education is started, others will follow, and restoration of America will greatly accelerate.

Pray about what your part may be in this process.

Many Ways to Be Involved:

1. Every gifting, every skill, every vocation, every profession, and every calling is needed to complete the Great Commission. What is important is that we set apart, or consecrate these things for service to God's purposes.
2. While some of you will be called to start new organizations and structures, there are many existing opportunities to serve with your skills and abilities, and to receive further training. You can get involved through church denominations, missionary agencies, medical and relief agencies, Bible translation agencies, and other avenues.
3. Expect God to show you things about what he has gifted you in, what you are interested in, and the

burdens you have felt for people, places, and languages.

4. If you are a student, the years of your study can be alive with a thrilling sense of purpose. Whether you are interested in law or linguistics, medicine or mechanics, business, banking, bookbinding or beekeeping…ask God how he is calling you to be educated to serve his purposes.
5. All of us are called to pray. You may feel called to lead prayer meetings as part of your church or among friends. The prayer room is in reality the engine room for spiritual breakthrough in the lives of individuals and in nations. "History is silent about revivals that did not begin with prayer," said evangelist and historian Dr. J Edwin Orr.
6. America is already an astoundingly generous nation. May that wonderful example continue. How can you, your family, your business, church or foundation give in strategic ways to help finish the Great Commission? Consider adopting an unreached people group with the goal of helping support missionary work among them. It would begin with prayer, and may involve exploratory trips and partnership with missionary agencies. If your business has believers on staff, a weekly prayer meeting could provide prayer and encouraging messages for the missionaries, and a time to hear reports from the field.
7. Languages needing Bible translation can be adopted too through prayer and support for those translating. (Please see Appendix C for relevant resources)
8. Many parts of the world need more hospitals, schools, and employment opportunities provided by those who have been called to show the compassion of God.
9. Begin a discipleship group for young people through your church, in your neighborhood, or for foreign students coming to attend university in the United States.

The points listed above are just a beginning. 20/20 Vision for America is about God showing us individually and corporately how the blessing he has given to America can be harnessed for his purposes—to be a blessing to "all the families of the earth."

NOTES:

1. *Christianity in its Global Context,* 1970–2020 Society, Religion, and Mission, Gordon Conwell Theological Seminary, 2013. Accessed 11/19/2019. https://archive.gordonconwell.edu/ockenga/research/documents/ChristianityinitsGlobalContext.pdf.
2. "World Population Clock: 7.7 Billion People (2019) – Worldometers". *www.worldometers.info.* Accessed 12/02/2019.
3. Joshua Project, https://joshuaproject.net/people_groups/statistics. Accessed 12/02/2019.
4. Ibid.
5. Ibid.
6. A range inclusive of estimates from multiple respected sources. Factors affecting this number include definitions of vital, active languages vs. languages no longer spoken as a mother tongue, languages being discovered, and languages beginning translation. For more information, visit: https://www.wycliffe.net/en/statistics.
7. Dana Robert, *Christian Mission: How Christianity Became a World Religion* (Chichester: Wiley-Blackwell, 2009).

12

Main Application—Point Three: Govern Yourself and Your Nation

From the Mayflower Compact: Having undertaken for the Glory of God, and Advancement of the Christian Faith...[we] solemnly and mutually, in the Presence of God and one another, covenant and combine ourselves together into a civil body politick, for our better ordering and preservation, and furtherance of the ends aforesaid: And...do enact, constitute, and frame, such just and equal Laws, Ordinances, Acts, Constitutions, and Officers...unto which we promise all due Submission and Obedience.

From Scripture: First of all, then, I urge that entreaties and prayers, petitions and thanksgivings, be made on behalf of all men, for kings and all who are in authority, so that we may lead a tranquil and quiet life in all godliness and dignity. (1 Timothy 2:1-2)

Crowns in the Gutter

Imagine, if in a moment of time your eyes were opened to see them—in every town and city, along the side of every country road—crowns, just lying in the gutter. Not cheap plastic imitations, but weighty crowns of precious metal and authentic gems.

For one moment you think you are in a dream. In the next, you think of the riches you could have if you gathered them up. But then reality rushes in with a chilling sense of unease. You see people on the sidewalk with their eyes glazed over, walking right past this treasure like it is trash. "Something is terribly wrong," you whisper to yourself. "Why is something so valuable lying in the gutter while nobody cares?"

Wishing by now it was just a dream, you finally see what has been going on. A young man with a backpack walks awkwardly past you, then stops. Something he had been given to carry has been bothering him. Visibly irritated, he opens his backpack, finding the cause of his discomfort—the points of a gleaming crown. With a look of disdain, he casts the crown into the gutter, crosses the street, and goes on his way.

Reality Check

There *are* crowns in the gutter in America.

"In free governments," said Benjamin Franklin, "the rulers are the servants and the people their superiors and sovereigns."[1] Sovereigns, like kings and queens, wear crowns. Beginning with the Mayflower Compact and culminating in the founding of the United States of America, the concept of the monarchy was turned upside down. As a result, we the people have been given—metaphorically—the crown of sovereignty. We have been given the privilege to rule ourselves.

This same Benjamin Franklin, as he departed from Independence Hall in Philadelphia at the conclusion of the Constitutional Convention in 1787, was approached regarding the form of government the founders had produced. One lady asked him bluntly, "Well, Doctor, what have we got—a Republic or a Monarchy?" His sobering answer was, "A Republic, if you can keep it."[2]

Have you cast your crown into the gutter?

"Keeping the republic" includes preserving our freedom of religion, freedom of speech, freedom to assemble, freedom of the press, and other vital freedoms. It means not just voting in elections, which is crucial, but actively promoting the preservation of the form of government that has ensured and protected these freedoms. To do this, we need to put on, so to speak, our crown of sovereignty and be responsible for governing ourselves and our nation.

You've Got it Good

Paul urges Christians to pray for government in 1 Timothy 2:1-2. The prescribed prayer is a request to be free to live a "tranquil and quiet life in all godliness." Notice that the prayer is to be able to live a life that expresses *all* godliness.

For the Pilgrims in England, there was very little expression of godliness that the government allowed. For just meeting together as a private church they were harassed and hounded by the authorities. But on the other side of the Atlantic, the Mayflower Compact explicitly granted them the answer to their own prayers for a "tranquil and quiet life in all godliness." Furthermore, the birth of the United States of America was an answer to that prayer for many others—on a truly massive scale.

"It Ain't Like This Everywhere"

As a missionary, I regularly meet people from backgrounds in extremely oppressive nations. If they visit America, they marvel at the religious freedom they see, where police, military, and government personnel are freely attending church services together. Their experience has been that government authorities are the ones stomping out liberty and religious expression.

In spite of significant erosion of this nation's foundations, America has still "got it good." We enjoy liberty that was dreamed of for thousands of years, and that many nations still dream of today.

But if America is to be known in the future as the "land of the free, and the home of the brave,"[3] then we need to take our responsibility for civil government seriously.

God and Liberty

It is a simple truth that references to God, the Bible, and the Christian faith permeated the foundational period of America. These topics sat comfortably with the Founding Fathers, even in their discussions about government. The pressure has been intense for many decades to recast America as a nation built on purely secular ideas. However, even a simple look at history, and a proper understanding of separation of church and state (civil government), will tell a different story.

Beginning with the Pilgrims, we can see that the Mayflower Compact of 1620 was a small-scale model of government designed to protect life and property, and to further God-given purposes. This concept of government developed throughout New England, as seen in other compacts such as The Fundamental Orders of Connecticut.[4] When America was born as a nation in 1776, the same idea is plainly stated in the Declaration of Independence:

> We hold these truths to be self-evident, that all men are created equal, that they are endowed by their Creator with certain unalienable Rights, that among these are Life, Liberty and the pursuit of Happiness.–That to secure these rights, Governments are instituted among Men, deriving their just powers from the consent of the governed...

Drafted in 1787, the United States Constitution describes itself in language that perfectly complements the Declaration of Independence. The following is from the Constitution's preamble:

> We the People of the United States, in Order to form a more perfect Union, establish Justice, insure domestic Tranquility, provide for the common defence, promote the general Welfare, and secure the Blessings of Liberty to

ourselves and our Posterity, do ordain and establish this Constitution for the United States of America.

Distinction Between Church and State

We looked earlier at the problems during the Medieval Period when church and state were essentially intertwined as one. We also saw how the Church of England—acting as an oppressive, government-controlled expression of Christianity—was the reason many were leaving England for North America. As a result, the Christians that shaped early America had a distaste for government running the church or administrating any kind of state-run denomination. They knew there was a distinction between the role of the church and that of the state.

When Scripture introduces the topic of civil government following Israel's departure from Egypt, we see even then a distinction between the roles of Moses and Aaron. Moses had a more governmental role, acting as a judge for settling disputes, while his brother Aaron was assigned the priestly duties. While there was a certain separation of these spheres, both Moses and Aaron still related to God. One was not secular and the other religious—they were just distinct functions.

Even Jesus, who stated that his kingdom was "not of this world," recognized the God-ordained authority of civil government while before Pontius Pilate.[5] He also taught his disciples to "Render to Caesar the things that are Caesar's, and to God the things that are God's."[6]

Two Entities, One Foundation

The Reformation brought these distinctions back into view, helping to disentangle the functioning of church and state. Both Martin Luther and John Calvin wrote and taught on the idea of there being "two kingdoms," one which is the domain of the church, the other the domain of civil government. Calvin wrote, "Man is under two kinds of government—one spiritual, by which the conscience is formed to piety and the service of God; the other political, by which a man is instructed in the duties of humanity and civility."[7] He further explained, "The church does not assume to itself what belongs to the magistrate; nor can the magistrate execute that which is executed by the Church."[8]

Calvin saw this distinction in Jesus' teaching, when he said, "You know that the rulers of the Gentiles lord it over them, and their great men exercise authority over them. It is not this way among you" (Matthew 20:25-26). While pointing out the difference between functions of church and state, Calvin nevertheless recognized that both sat on the same foundation of truth revealed in Scripture. He stated, "all laws are preposterous which neglect the claims of God, and merely provide for the interests of men."[9]

John Locke

This understanding of the distinction between church and civil government continued to develop, while maintaining biblical foundations for civil government. John Locke, the 17th-century philosopher who greatly influenced the Founding Fathers, believed government should not coerce people into religious conformity, yet he constantly reconciled his views on government to the Bible. The Pilgrims, with their Mayflower Compact, stated that their goals were clearly religious, but created their civil government separately from their church government. The Declaration of Independence recognized that rights come from God, and that government exists to protect these rights, yet paved the way for a Constitution that was purposefully opposed to the administration of a state denomination. "Separation of church and state," for the founders of America was clearly not the same thing as "separation of state from Judeo-Christian foundations."

Legislating Morality?

To see the importance of both separation of church and

state, *and* Judeo-Christian foundations for government, ask yourself the following question: Can morality be legislated? Many people answer "No, you can't force someone to be moral." They are right in one sense, but there is more to it. If morality cannot be legislated, what then are lawmakers supposed to legislate? The truth is, the only thing that ought to be legislated is morality! The real question is, "Which aspects of morality are the domain of government, and which are the domain of the church?"

The founders knew that the biblical prohibitions against murder and theft have direct relevance to the purpose of civil government and to the laws necessary for a free nation. They knew Scripture's prohibition against lying was a fundamental element in the administration of justice. However, they did not extend government's reach to those topics that are rightfully the church's to administer, such as learning to love God, the forgiveness for sins, communion, and so on.

Once we see this clearly, we can make major progress toward strengthening the foundation of America without confusing and entangling the related, but distinct entities of the church and civil government.

A Rare Form of Freedom

America's founding documents describe a historically rare form of liberty.

The famous hymn "It Is Well with My Soul" beautifully describes the internal peace and freedom that is possible through trusting God—even in the midst of suffering. Yet for those suffering under tyranny, it may be well with their soul, but it is not well with their city, state, or nation.

Internal peace and freedom are wonderful things, but the Mayflower Compact and America's founding documents were designed to secure the added dimension of *external* liberty.

For the Pilgrims, their experience under oppressive rule in England led them to pursue and appreciate this idea of external liberty. They wanted to be free to serve God to the fullest potential, something they could not do in England. Hungering for what is good and right is something Jesus commended, saying, "Blessed are those who hunger and thirst for righteousness, for they shall be satisfied" (Matthew 5:6).

We need to be like that today. Like the Pilgrims before them, America's founders were greatly interested in understanding what it would take to attain the fullness of liberty. They were well versed in the historical development of political thought, as evidenced by Thomas Jefferson's part in writing the Declaration of Independence.

In a letter to James Madison, Jefferson stated, "Whether I had gathered my ideas from reading or reflection I do not know. I know only that I turned to neither book nor pamphlet while writing it."[10] However, compare the similarities between a passage in John Locke's famous "Two Treatises of Government," published in 1689, and the wording of the Declaration:

> **John Locke:** "But if a long train of abuses, prevarications, and artifices, all tending the same way, make the design visible to the people…it is not to be wondered at that they should then rouze themselves and endeavour to put the rule into such hands which may secure to them the ends for which government was at first erected"[11]

> **The Declaration:** "But when a long train of abuses and usurpations, pursuing invariably the same object evinces a design to reduce them under absolute despotism, it is their right, it is their duty, to throw off such government, and to provide new guards for their future security…"

For Jefferson and others of his time, the ideas of people like John Locke were so well known they could be recalled and applied without looking them up.

Let My People Go!

Are we, like the Pilgrims and Founders, hungry for liberty? Or are we indifferent toward it, or worse still have we given up on it? Perhaps, if you are a Christian, you have never thought that good government is glorifying to God, and that it advances his purposes in the earth. The same God who confronted Pharaoh saying, "Let my people go!" has now called his people to "go into all the world." God had to secure liberty for the Israelites so they could go on their journey to the promised land. God has blessed America with liberty so that we can go on a journey too—bringing the gospel into every land.

Good government should matter to us. It matters to God. "Righteousness and justice are the foundation of [his] throne" (Psalm 89:14).

Treasuring What We Have

As we have seen in our short stroll through history, it took a long time for elements of "righteousness and justice" to make their way into the foundations of civil government. The truths embedded in the foundations of America's government are of inestimable value. Some examples are:

- Our fundamental rights (Life, Liberty, Property) come from God, and not man. They do not change with the shifting sands of opinion or culture.
- We belong to God, not man or the state. Our value is intrinsic, and not determined by our usefulness to the state.
- Government rightfully exists to protect the God-given rights and purposes of the people—the people do not exist to serve the government.
- We are the government! We were given a government of the people, by the people, and for the people.

The High Cost of Doing Nothing

Think about what we will *not* be able to do if America loses the God-given liberty we have been entrusted with. We would not be free to meet together in churches of our choosing, to establish seminaries, Bible schools, and missionary training programs. We would not be free to leave America, taking our money with us to serve God's purposes throughout the world. We would not be able to fulfill the vision the Pilgrims had, of "laying good foundations, or at least of making some way towards it, for the propagation and advance of the gospel of the kingdom of Christ in the remote parts of the world."

But favorable government multiplies the opportunities the church has for reaching the world. We can observe this as a historical fact. America has been a missionary sending epicenter for over two hundred years now. As noted in the previous chapter, America sent 127,000 of the approximately 400,000 missionaries sent out worldwide in 2010. The next closest nation sent 34,000.[12] These statistics don't just happen by accident.

Another "Great Experiment"

Yes, the church can strengthen and grow under persecution. But why should America wait until all liberty has been lost to decide to strengthen and grow? Why not conduct another "Great Experiment," and see what happens when believers in this nation return to their deepest foundations—living for the glory of God, advancing the Christian faith, and being responsible for civil government? I say let's do that instead!

Appeal to Heaven

We need to take heart that America was certainly not built by the efforts of wise leaders alone. Both the Pilgrims and the Founding Fathers knew that God himself was involved in the process, something they called Divine Providence. For the Pilgrims, this included the provision of their friendship with Samoset, Squanto, and Massasoit—Native Americans who helped them practically and in their relationship to other native peoples.

The Founding Fathers saw constant evidence of divine

favor for their cause, as George Washington described in his inaugural address, "No People can be bound to acknowledge and adore the invisible hand, which conducts the affairs of men more than the People of the United States. Every step, by which they have advanced to the character of an independent nation, seems to have been distinguished by some token of providential agency."[13] Jesus taught us to pray, "Your kingdom come. Your will be done, on earth as it is in heaven." Corrupt, tyrannous government does not rule in heaven! Therefore, we can pray and work toward restoring the original intention of the Constitution, with "firm reliance on the protection of Divine Providence."[14]

Ways You Can Be Involved:

1. As mentioned in the previous chapter, we must pray. Paul said "First of all, then, I urge that entreaties and prayers, petitions and thanksgivings, be made on behalf of all men, for kings and all who are in authority (1 Timothy 2:1-2).
2. Qualify yourself for liberty by governing yourself under God's law first of all. John Adams said, "Our Constitution was made only for a moral and religious People. It is wholly inadequate to the government of any other."[15]
3. Vote. You are part of the government of America. Remember the quote from Benjamin Franklin, "In free governments, the rulers are the servants and the people their superiors and sovereigns."[16]
4. Understand what the founding fathers were aiming for as they structured this nation's government in the form of the Constitution. Read the Constitution, study it, and be able to teach it.
5. Participate—beyond voting—in the political process. This is our privilege. The following are some examples. You can run for, and if elected, hold public office. You can call, write, or email your Senator or Representative

to inform them of how you would like them to represent you in Congress. You can even, when warranted, propose an idea to your Senator or Representative for a bill that could ultimately be signed into law.

6. Do the work only the church can do—the evangelism and discipleship that produces self-governed citizens who preserve, rather than reject, America's Judeo-Christian foundations.
7. Study the history of the church and state relationship. It is a very important topic to this day. Be able to inform people that America has foundations from our Judeo-Christian heritage that are essential—yet we are not seeking a theocracy.
8. Use this book to lead a small group at your church or your home.
9. Lastly, consider conducting a series of home meetings or classes, or a retreat or conference in which an understanding of the Constitution can be taught. Envision a new generation that understands the importance of liberty, not just for us, but for fulfilling God's purposes in the earth. Be part of raising up such a generation. There are excellent resources available in written and video format to facilitate this. See the Appendix C for details.
10. Renew the Covenant. As an individual, family, small group, or church body, take a pledge to renew the covenant made by our forefathers. See Appendix A – Renew the Covenant for details.

NOTES:

1. Benjamin Franklin, as quoted by Dr. James McHenry, in *The American Historical Review, Vol. XI* (New York: The MacMillan Company, 1906), 618.
2. Benjamin Franklin, *"Convention debate"* (Philadelphia, Pennsylvania, July 26, 1787).
3. Francis Scott Key, *"Star Spangled Banner,"* (Adopted as the United States National Anthem, March 3, 1931).

4. F. Newton Thorpe, *The Federal and State Constitutions, Colonial Charters, and Other Organic Laws of the State, Territories, and Colonies Now or Heretofore Forming the United States of America* (Washington: Government Printing Office, 1909).
5. John 19:11.
6. Mark 12:17.
7. John Calvin, *Institutes of the Christian Religion, translated by John Allen, in two volumes, Vol. II* (Philadelphia: Presbyterian Board of Education, 1844), 73-74.
8. Ibid, 398.
9. Ibid, 641.
10. Thomas Jefferson, *"From Thomas Jefferson to James Madison, 30 August 1823,"* Founders Online, National Archives, accessed September 29, 2019, https://founders.archives.gov/documents/Jefferson/98-01-02-3728.
11. Locke, John, *Two Treatises of Government* (London: Whitmore and Fenn, C. Brown, 1821), 382.
12. *Christianity in its Global Context, 1970–2020, Society, Religion, and Mission*, Gordon Conwell Theological Seminary, 2013, accessed November 19, 2019, https://archive.gordonconwell.edu/ockenga/research/documents/ChristianityinitsGlobalContext.pdf.
13. George Washington, *"Inaugural Address"* (speech, New York City, New York, April 30, 1789), National Archives, accessed December 18, 2019, https://www.archives.gov/exhibits/american_originals/inaugtxt.html.
14. *The Declaration of Independence,* 1776.
15. John Adams, *"From John Adams to Massachusetts Militia, 11 October 1798,"* Founders Online, National Archives, accessed September 29, 2019, https://founders.archives.gov/documents/Adams/99-02-02-3102.
16. Franklin, "Convention debate," 1787.

13

20/20 Vision for America

"Write the vision and make it plain on tablets, that he may run who reads it." (Habakkuk 2:2 NKJV)

It is exciting to think about the future. The human imagination has proven almost prophetic in its ability to see today what will appear tomorrow.

Wouldn't you love to step back in time to show Benjamin Franklin your smart phone, or tell the Pilgrims about crossing the Atlantic in less than eight hours? If that were possible, what would you really be saying to these forefathers? Would it be, "Hey, look how smart we are in the future?" Heaven forbid! On the contrary, you would be complementing the wisdom of their generations, saying, "Look at what has been built on the foundations your generation laid down!"

While there is much more to the success of a nation than technological advances, you may be wondering, "Why is a book about vision for America not focused on fusion reactors, travel to Mars, and the cure for every disease?" Well, actually, it is—indirectly.

Why is it that America has brought so many technological

advances to the world? It's worth thinking about because strictly speaking, necessity is not the mother of invention. If that were true, the poorest, most enslaved nations on earth would routinely be solving their own problems and lifting themselves out of need. The problem for these nations is not the lack of intelligence or inventiveness—it is a lack of liberty. They do not have the roots of liberty that we have, and therefore they aren't experiencing the fruit of liberty that we experience.

An Atmosphere of Advancement

A very special environment is created when an individual, a family, a business, a noble endeavor and even a nation is built on a foundation of truth. With the building blocks of character and purpose, and the fresh air of liberty to breathe, dreams can turn into realities. We have seen the mystery of flight get solved, footsteps appear on the moon, and so much more.

But far surpassing these wonders is the grand narrative playing out through history. God is at work to bring about the "restoration of all things" (Acts 3:21). This includes the restoration of our relationship with him and with one another. It is the restoration of truth about who we are, where we came from, and what our purpose is. It even includes the restoration of our understanding about government, and how we are to govern. Although imperfect and incomplete, the importance of America's part in this story has been on display for a watching world.

The World is Watching

Many are still watching—and wondering, "What will become of the nation that built on the self-evident truth that God is the source of our rights, and that government exists to protect them?" In a very real way, they are watching you and me.

America is at a tipping point.

The pressure is on right now for *we the people* to just fall in line—and to walk in lockstep with global groupthink. "You'll get whatever rights we decide you get!" is the attitude of many global elites, who have long despised the notion of unchanging rights given by a loving God. They are the modern face of the very tyranny from which America escaped.

In our age of globalism, it is more important than ever to preserve and strengthen the truth that a sovereign nation—a people bound together by their own consent—is a legitimate and essential entity on the world stage. History screams at us that handing over sovereignty to a centralized power is a disastrous course to follow.

But take heart.

Four centuries ago, our friends the Pilgrims helped turn the world around with three powerful ideas. As William Bradford recorded, their light shone brightly in the darkness:

> As one small candle may light a thousand, so the light enkindled here has shone to many, yea, in a sense to our whole nation; let the glorious name of Jehovah have all the praise.

Will you shine that same light in America today? With every beat of your heart the history of this generation is being written. What will the legacy be? Will it be the all too common story of pleasure over purpose, comfort over courage, or indulgence over inheritance? It does not have to be.

Patriotism is not just a feeling, it is also a responsibility. The root Latin word in *patriotism* is "pater," referring to "father." A father or mother has the responsibility of protecting, instructing, correcting, encouraging, and inspiring—the very things America as a nation needs right now.

God Bless America

America has been blessed—to be a blessing to the world. May that flourish and continue as we resolve to live for the glory of God, to advance the Christian faith, and to be responsible for civil government.

May a free, noble, and glorious future be seen, with "20/20 vision for America."

Appendix A: Renew the Covenant

The Mayflower Renewal Covenant

I hereby recognize that in 1620, a covenant was made between God and the passengers onboard the Mayflower, affirming that their journey to the New World was for the purposes of living for the glory of God and the advancement of the Christian faith, and that their modeling of self-government under God was to ensure the liberty to pursue those purposes.

I ________________________ choose to remember and renew the heart of this covenant by:

Living for the Glory of God

By examining my life in the light of Scripture, being transformed by renewing my mind, and by thinking of and living for whatever is true, honorable, right, pure, lovely, of good repute—anything that is excellent and worthy of praise. (Philippians 4:8)

Living for the Advancement of the Christian Faith

By remembering that we have been blessed with the knowledge of God, his gifts of life, liberty, wealth, influence, and education so that we would be a blessing to all the peoples of the earth—fulfilling Jesus' command to "Go therefore and make disciples of all the nations, baptizing them in the name of the Father and the Son and the Holy Spirit, teaching them to observe all that I commanded you" (Matthew 28:19-20).

Being Responsible for Civil Government

By first of all governing myself, then fulfilling my God-given duty to teach self-government to my children, and then participating in the promotion of limited civil government that leaves people free to lead quiet and peaceable lives in all godliness (1 Timothy 2:3).

Signature: ____________________________ **Date:** __________

This covenant can also be downloaded in printable form, suitable for framing and placing on your wall. Go to: 2020vfa.com/sign

Appendix B: Training Opportunities

Having worked as a staff member of YWAM Tyler since 1995, I would like to recommend the following training opportunities as you pray about making application to the message of this book.

— Chris Lascelles

FOR TEENAGERS

Season of Service and Training (SST)
SST is YWAM Tyler's discipleship and missions training program for teenagers. This two-week summer course is for 13 – 17 year olds. One week of dynamic worship, teaching and team building is followed by a week of adventure, reaching out to others across the country. See sst.org for details.

FOR AGE 18 AND OVER

See ywamtyler.org for details on the following schools

Discipleship Training School (DTS)
DTS is YWAM's point of entry school, designed to bring you—the messenger—into a closer relationship with God. Along with people from many other nations, you will learn about who God is, what his character is like, who you are made to be, how to have healthy relationships, world missions, worship, prayer, and more. Three months of training are followed by six weeks of field trips to locations all over the world.

SECONDARY SCHOOLS

Completion of DTS required. Like the DTS, all YWAM schools have an outreach phase—for putting into practice what has been learned.

School of Evangelism (SOE)
SOE is about seeing the world through God's eyes. Designed to equip the messenger with what is needed for making God known to others—the message. SOE imparts a biblical worldview, and the ability to communicate the Christian faith to other cultures and

communities around the world. SOE is about greater preparation for the task of "making disciples of all nations" (Matthew 28:19).

The School of Strategic Missions (SOSM)

SOSM is specialized training for taking the gospel to the hard places of the world. This school takes your calling and vision and turns it into an actionable plan. Providing more than just knowledge, SOSM helps with preparing a team and building a support structure for successfully pioneering a new work.

School of Worship (SOW)

SOW calls musicians and non-musicians alike to gaze on the beauty and character of God—then lead others to so the same. SOW imparts a lifestyle of worship, the study of scripture, and leadership skills, along with basic elements of audio and video production.

Teachers for the Nations (TFN)

TFN is a one-year teacher training program that prepares Christian teachers to equip children and adults to take leadership in the spheres that shape a nation—family, church, government, education, business, arts and entertainment, and media. TFN graduates have successfully started schools in many nations of the world.

Communication and Culture Course (CCC)

CCC is for non-native English speakers looking to get a solid grip on English—especially those wanting to feel confident to attend DTS and further YWAM training. This school provides a learning environment of interaction with native English speakers in the classroom, at work, and at play.

Appendix C: Resources

Websites:

For Training:
Youth With A Mission (YWAM) - ywam.org
YWAM Tyler - ywamtyler.org

For getting the Bible into every language on earth:
End Bible Poverty Now - endbiblepovertynow.com

For understanding America's Christian heritage:
Wall Builders - wallbuilders.com

For statistics on global Christianity and missions:
Joshua Project - joshuaproject.net

Books:

Loren Cunningham, *Is That Really You, God?*
Vishal Mangalwadi, *The Book That Made Your World: How The Bible Created The Soul Of Western Civilization*

Video:

David Barton and Rick Green, *Constitution Alive! A Citizen's Guide to the Constitution.* Available on Amazon or at shop.wallbuilders.com

Made in the USA
Las Vegas, NV
09 November 2020